Thomas Schirrmacher

The Koran and the Bible

"World of Theology Series"

Studies published by the Theological Commission of the World Evangelical Alliance

Vol 7

Vol 1   Thomas K. Johnson: The First Step in Missions Training: How our Neighbors are Wrestling with God's General Revelation
Vol 2   Thomas K. Johnson: Christian Ethics in Secular Cultures
Vol 3   David Parker: Discerning the Obedience of Faith: A Short History of the World Evangelical Alliance Theological Commission
Vol 4   Thomas Schirrmacher (Ed.): William Carey: Theologian – Linguist – Social Reformer
Vol 5   Thomas Schirrmacher: Advocate of Love – Martin Bucer as Theologian and Pastor
Vol 6   Thomas Schirrmacher: Culture of Shame / Culture of Guilt
Vol 7   Thomas Schirrmacher: The Koran and the Bible
         (This book is also available in German and Turkish) Vol 8   Thomas Schirrmacher (Ed.): The Humanisation of Slavery in the Old Testament
Vol 9   Jim Harries: New Foundations for Appreciating Africa: Beyond Religious and Secular Deceptions
Vol 10   Thomas Schirrmacher: Missio Dei – God's Missional Nature
Vol 11   Thomas Schirrmacher: Biblical Foundations for 21st Century World Mission

Thomas Schirrmacher

The Koran and the Bible

translated by Richard McClary

revised by Thomas K. Johnson

WIPF & STOCK · Eugene, Oregon

Wipf and Stock Publishers
199 W 8th Ave, Suite 3
Eugene, OR 97401

The Koran and the Bible
By Schirrmacher, Thomas
Copyright©2013 Verlag für Kultur und Wissenschaft
ISBN 13: 978-1-5326-5576-0
Publication date 4/17/2018
Previously published by Verlag für Kultur und Wissenschaft, 2013

Contents

I. The Bible and the Koran as "God's Word": How They are Understood as Revelation and Inspiration 7
"Putting it in a Nutshell" Leads to Some Limitations 7
A Comparison of How the Two Holy Scriptures View
    Themselves 9
Sent from Heaven or Developed over the Millennia? 11
A Book or a Collection of Writings? 13
Holy and Perfect Language or Functional Language? 14
Is Holy Language Effectual if not Understood, or is Proclamation
    Required in Order to Lead to Better Understanding? 16
Can Translations be "God's Word?" 18
Literal or Actual Meaning? The Letter or the Spirit? 20
A Uniform and Holy Style or a Variety of Styles? 21
Were the Authors Passive Recipients or were Their Personalities
    Actively Involved? 21
A Divine Style or do the Authors have Numerous Styles? 24
A Timeless Text or is History Central? 25
Timeless Validity or a Validity Found in the Development of the
    Plan of Salvation? 27
Veneration of the Printed Copy or Use as a Basic Object of Utility? 29
Superiority or Self-Criticism? 30
Faith: Submission or Trust with Lament and Doubt? 33
Scholarly Treatment: Is it There to Defend the Scriptures or to
    Better Understand Them? 34
Textual Criticism – Yes or No? 36

II. A Relationship With God and How it Emerges Through His Word 43
Has God Revealed Himself? 43
Faith as Recognition of the Lordship of God, or Faith as a Mutual
    Relationship of Trust? 45
Is God Free from Obligation or Bound to His Promises? 47
A Prohibition Against Testing God or a Challenge to Test God? ... 49
Is Love God's Reaction or is it the Deepest Indication of His
    Nature? 50
God: Lord or Friend and Brother? 53
The Founder of the Religion: Warlord or Peacemaker? 53

The Founder of the Religion: Master or Servant?...............................55
Is Prayer above All a Communal Duty or a Personal Conversation
    with the Father?...55
Koran or Jesus? A Book or a Person?..57
Is the Founder Above or Beneath the Holy Scriptures?....................58
A Celebration for the Holy Scriptures?...60
Jesus: Prophet or God and Provider of Salvation?............................60
The Trinity: Polytheism or the Nature of God? 63
Excursus: How God comes near according to the Bible...................65
Is Sin Committed only Against People or Above All Against God?..66
Is Sin an Isolated Act or is Original Sin the Foundational Rupture
    in the Relationship with God?..67
Does Conversion Occur by Confession or by Receipt of
    Salvation?...69
The Central Theme of the Holy Scriptures: is it Submission or
    Salvation?...69
Does Forgiveness come by Obedience or by the Reconciling
    Action of God?...70
Submission or Reconciliation?..71

III. Aids for Further Study 73
How can Christians Best Speak with Muslims?................................73

Literature for Further Study...77
Non-Muslim Editions of the Koran and Non-Muslim Commentaries......... 77
Muslim Editions of the Koran and Muslim Commentaries......................... 77
Muslim Works on the Koran und Islam 77
Nonaligned and Academic Works Regarding the Koran and Islam 78
Dictionaries on Islam 79
Nonaligned and Academic Works Comparing the Bible and the Koran 80
Christian Works on the Koran and Islam and Comparisons of the Bible
    and the Koran 80
Editions of the Bible 81
Muslim Works on the Bible and Christianity 81
Introductions to the Bible and Christianity... 81
On the Historical and Contemporary Relationship between Islam and
    Christianity 82

About the Author...83

I. The Bible and the Koran as "God's Word": How They are Understood as Revelation and Inspiration

"Putting it in a Nutshell" Leads to Some Limitations

The challenge in composing this book lies in its brevity. What follows addresses the two largest world religions, the followers of which make up over half of the world's population. Both religions are also fragmented into innumerable groups, such that it would not be possible to name them all. Additionally, the book seeks to introduce and compare the two most often translated and most influential books in history, the contents of which cannot easily be summarized in an abbreviated manner.

	Percentage of the World Population	**Followers**	**Annual Growth**
Christianity	33 %	2.0 bn.	+ 1.43 %
Islam	21 %	1.3 bn.	+ 2.17 %
Total	100 %	7.05 bn.[1]	+ 1.39 %

One can compare Islam and Christianity by asking what it is that is most important to each of them. This can be done by systematically setting up their teachings alongside each other and by asking what each says about the other, by examining their individual histories or their historical relationship to each other, or by asking how they address current issues such as human rights, the role of women, and missions. Even if all the aforementioned appears in some form in this book, the way that has been chosen is another. It is a way that has seldom been chosen, namely the way revelation is understood in the principal documents of these two religions.

That naturally means that the historical development of both religions can only be slightly addressed, and that the preponderance of attention must be given to the holy writings and to the founders Mohammed and Jesus. That naturally also means that as far as Islam is concerned, only that which is common to all Muslims can be addressed. Theological differences

---

[1] 01.01.2013 (http://www.census.gov/population/popclockworld.html)

between Sunnis and Shi'ites, for example, or the cultural differences between Arabian, Persian, Turkish and Asian Islam cannot be addressed. The *Hadith*, the tradition relating to the words and deeds of Mohammed and his early followers and the corresponding way of life of the Sunna are mentioned but nowhere developed as a central theme.

The same applies to Christianity. Only rarely will something be mentioned that is not common to all Christian confessions and that has not been traditionally shared throughout the centuries. However, this leads to the fact that views, for example, particular to the Roman Catholic emphasis on the role of the church for salvation, or the fact that Orthodox churches saw themselves to be obligated to the early Church Fathers, will appear as little as the enormous historical and cultural diversity of Christianity. Likewise, the wide variety of opinion in "modern" theology, be it in historico-critical or evangelical garb, can simply not be taken up in this work.

Furthermore, the view that, in our opinion, Judaism is seminal for Christianity, will be ignored. This means that the Old Testament will exclusively be presented in its New Testament and Christian understanding, as desirous as a broader approach might be.

This book often presents the dogmatic consensus found in churches prior to the onset of modernity, passing over the intra-Christian critiques of dogma and biblical criticism that have been discussed since the 18th century. This is due to lack of space as well as the fact that otherwise the actual focus of the book would be lost. To address such issues as the theological historico-critical questions would have only widened the differences between Islam and Christianity with regard to holy writings. At the same time it is therefore easy to cover up the fact that differences with regard to handling Holy Scriptures in Islam and Christianity are much more than one thousand years old. **My concern is to show that the differences between Islam and Christianity lie in the understanding of the holy books and how they are employed in the life of "the faithful."**

This can all be said differently: This book concentrates so much on the significant aspects in Islam and Christianity from the standpoint of their origins and from the understanding of their primary documents that it deals with a precise train of thought in a brief manner. The book purposely dispenses with many other topics of current interest such as were included in some depth in the "Clarity and Being a Good Neighbor" handout from the Evangelical Church in Germany.[2] At the same time it can also be said that

---

[2] *Klarheit und gute Nachbarschaft: Christen und Muslime in Deutschland: Eine Handreichung des Rates der EKD.* Kirchenamt der EKD: Hannover, 2006; (Download see Bibliography).

this book foregoes comment on political and social dimensions. Rather, it has to do with basics and connecting notions that have held all groups together throughout the centuries. The respective political implementations in the past and present would require a much more comprehensive treatise.

The presuppositions that I, as a Christian, act on when in conversation with a Muslim are elaborated in the practical part of the book (Part III). This book was written by a Christian, and the fact that it endorses the Christian point of view is not concealed. However, I have made every effort to correctly and fairly present the Muslim position. I hope that Muslims, even if they do not value the orientation of this book, will find that in spite of this fact their concept of God and their understanding of the Koran is the one they actually know and live out.

According to the Eighth Commandment, Muslims also have the right to be protected from false witness. There are too many serious topics of discussion between Christians and Muslims for additional problems to be caused by rumors and defamatory statements. In my book *Concept of an Enemy – Islam*,[3] I have taken up and demonstrated the extent to which much of what is said regarding Islam is slanderous on the basis of numerous topics using the splinter political party "The Christian Middle" as an example.

Throughout the book I consistently use the designation "God" for Islam and for Christianity. I also do not specifically use *Allah* for the God of Islam. This is due to the fact that I assume that the word *Allah* stems from the old Near Eastern (and Old Testament) word *El* for God and that *Allah* is simply the Arabian expression for "God." Likewise, in my book *Concept of an Enemy – Islam* I have documented in detail that long before Mohammed, Arab Christians prayed to *Allah*, for example in the Arabian translation of the Apostles' creed in the 4th century.

A Comparison of How the Two Holy Scriptures View Themselves

If one compares the major world religions in which a single book plays a central role as Holy Scripture and "God's word," it demonstrates that the understanding of the respective books could hardly be more different. *"The word of God" is not the same thing as "The word of God."* **Stated differently: The fundamental difference between Christianity and Islam can**

---

[3] Thomas Schirrmacher, *Feindbild Islam: Am Beispiel der Partei „Christliche Mitte"*, VTR: Nürnberg, 2003, esp. pp. 76-95.

be highlighted in the respective traditional (that is to say, pre-critical) understandings of their holy books. The notions of this book are predicated on this basic thought. For the sake of brevity we will consciously limit ourselves in various respects.

First, I would like to consciously leave the question of criticism of the historical creditability of the Koran and the Bible aside. With respect to the Bible I am only looking for how the biblical authors and texts view themselves and for the understanding of the Scriptures held by churches before the onset of modern biblical criticism. This 'self-image' actually demonstrates why later biblical criticism emerged in the first place in the Christian (and Jewish) realms, while there was and is no similar development in Islam. Stated differently, as far as the Bible is concerned, the following comparison describes above all the present evangelical position (or from the viewpoint of Roman Catholicism the position of the Second Vatican Council's dei verbum revelatory decree). Since this conservative understanding of inspiration is already so strongly different from the Muslim viewpoint, then for dissenting Christians it will be even more the case that their modern understanding of the Bible differs from the Muslim understanding of the Koran.

Secondly, I consciously ignore questioning formulated doctrines. Take, for example, a belief in Islam that the Koran is unhistorical. This means that the Koran has no relationship to the life story of Mohammed because it had always been in finished form in heaven. We will leave this as it stands, even if western Islamic Studies and Christian criticism views this differently. For instance, this topic could look at exceptions that were only granted to Mohammed in the Koran and correspond to a particular life situation (e.g., more than four wives, marriage at a younger age, war in times of peace treaties).[4] For the life story and the concerns of Jesus, I follow the New Testament gospels completely independently of the discussion of what exactly we can know about Jesus historically.[5]

Thirdly, I largely ignore presenting how Islam's and Christianity's statements about each other judge each other. This is done as long as it does not arise directly out of the issue at hand, for example in the case of where the roles of Jesus in the Bible and in the Koran are compared. For

---

[4] See for instance the arguments in Eberhard *Troeger's* „Offenbarung Allahs oder Worte Muhammads? Zum Problem der Geschichtlichkeit des Korans" in: *Islam und christlicher Glaube* 5 (2005), pp. 16-22 and Steven *Masood, The Bible and the Quran: A Question of Integrity*, Carlisle: OM, 2001.

[5] See *Benedikt XVI* – Joseph Ratzinger, *Jesus von Nazareth: Von der Taufe im Jordan bis zur Verklärung*, Freiburg: Herder, 2007.

instance, I do not address the Muslim allegation that there is document falsification (Arabian tharif) and that the Jewish and Christian documents differ from those of the Koran because in the course of the centuries the former documents have been changed.

Fourthly, the brevity of this book does not allow all statements to be documented in detail with verses from the Bible or the Koran or from all other available documents. That it is often a matter of discretion as to when I document something or not goes without saying. In any event, in the following the intention is that no disputed statements having to do with either religion should be made but that only those statements to which a "Bible-believing" Christian or a "Koran-believing" Muslim would hold.

The structure of each section is with some exception consistent throughout the book. Initially, after each heading, there are two theses in italicized print which compare the views of the Bible and the Koran. Thereafter there is a thorough presentation of the perspective of the Koran, followed by a corresponding view regarding the Bible.

Sent from Heaven or Developed over the Millennia?

*According to the Muslim notion, the **Koran** is timeless, preserved eternally in heaven and over a period of 22 years "sent down" as a finished revelation. It was only received by Mohammed and passed down via recitation. God is the sole author of the Koran.*

The **Bible** arose over a very long period of time within the framework of human history. Its divine inspiration does not change the fact that it is first of all a product of history and it is not to be understood apart from its historical development. People set in historical circumstances are the authors of the Bible; by the Holy Spirit divine biblical authorship makes its marvelous appearance.

According to Islamic theology and how the **Koran** sees itself, the Koran as revealed to Mohammed in the 22 years between 610 and 632 A.D. had always existed with God in its original version in heaven. Revelation took place in that a finished specimen of the document, the "mother of the book" or "mother book" (Arabic um al kitab, comp. Sura 43,2-4; 56,78), was read out to Mohammed, mediated by the angel Gabriel. In 610 A.D. Mohammed (569/570-632 A.D.) began to proclaim Islam in the city of Mecca after receiving inspiration on Mount Hira near Mecca. The angel Gabriel requested that he "recite" a message from God (Arabic qara'a, therefore Quran = "reading," or "recitation").

That the Koran was not composed by mankind and also not in the 7th century, but that rather an already existent text was sent down, belong to the most frequently made statements in the Koran (e. g. Suras 2:176,185; 3:3,7; 4:47,136,166; 5:102; 6:92.155; 7:2,3; 14:1; 17:105; 18:2; 21:50; 25:6,32; 29:51; 38:29; 39:23; 42:17; 44:3; 65:10). "According to the Muslim faith, the historical book based on Mohammed's prophetic proclamation goes back to a heavenly record, as is the case with all true testimony of revelation. This is the eternal norm for all instances of proclamation of 'God's word' in the world. The reliability of the Koran of history has its foundation in a heavenly original that cannot be falsified. The fact that it is a 'revelation' of God is expressed in a metaphor of the Koran: 'It is an outpouring from the Lord of all the world' (Sura 26:192). The 'mother script' does not have a meaning on its own but rather as a communication of God to mankind: Mohammed's prophetic messages should not be considered his human word, but rather truly God's word (Sura 46:10)."[6]

According to the **Bible**'s notion of itself, and within the view held throughout the history of Christian theology, the Bible was not produced in heaven. Rather, it was composed over a period of one thousand-five hundred years. The Bible did not fall from heaven and was not in one form or another existent in heaven. It was written by people. Before a text emerged or was composed, and the attendant revelation occurred (for instance to an Old Testament prophet), the corresponding text did not exist anywhere. Even prior to the time of biblical criticism, the inspiration of the Bible meant that God revealed himself to people in history. He also guarded the process of recording the testimonies, reports and thoughts of the relevant people so that at the same time what was written by people and what emerged within history as texts proclaims God's eternal and divine message in unadulterated form. Christian churches have at all times understood inspiration to mean that God is not the sole author of Scripture. Rather, it has been understood that he came to the human authors in a wondrous and indefinable way by the Holy Spirit.

The World Catechism of the Catholic Church[7] writes the following in characteristic fashion by including the formulation of the Dogmatic Constitution of Divine Revelation Dei Verbum (DV) from the Second Vatican Council: "The inspired books teach the truth. 'Since therefore all that the inspired authors or sacred writers affirm should be regarded as affirmed by

---

[6] Hans Zirker, *Der Koran*, Primus: Darmstadt 1999¹; 2007², p. 44.
[7] http://www.usccb.org/catechism/text/pt1sect1chpt2.htm or http://www.vatican.va/archive/hist_councils/ii_vatican_council/documents/vat-ii_const_19651118_dei-verbum_en.html.

the Holy Spirit, we must acknowledge that the books of Scripture firmly, faithfully, and without error teach that truth which God, for the sake of our salvation, wished to see confided to the Sacred Scriptures'" (DV 11). It immediately adds the following: "God inspired the human authors of the sacred books. 'To compose the sacred books, God chose certain men who, all the while he employed them in this task, made full use of their own faculties and powers so that, though he acted in them and by them, it was as true authors that they consigned to writing whatever he wanted written, and no more.'" (DV11, §107 and §106).

A Book or a Collection of Writings?

*The **Koran** arose in a short time. It is a self-contained book that was revealed to a single person and presents a unity in linguistic, literary, historical, geographical, and ethnological respects.*

The **Bible** is actually not a book but rather a collection of 66 different writings (books) from different times and regions and presents texts from almost one thousand-five hundred years in diverse linguistic, literary, historical, geographical, and ethnological respects.

In its finished form the **Koran** was existent in heaven and made its way to Mohammed in the relatively short period of 22 years, even though the period of time to collect what was initially passed down orally extended over a longer period of time. The Koran is understood as a cohesive revelation in the same language, with the same style and the same concern and under the same time circumstances. (The length of the Koran roughly corresponds to that of the New Testament.)

In contrast the **Bible** was originally called bibloi, i.e., "rolls," "books" or "collection of books." Not until Medieval Latin was the designation changed from the plural to the singular biblia ("book," "Bible"). Matthew 26:56 and Romans 16:26 speak of the "writings of the prophets." John 5:46-47 refers to "what [Moses] wrote," 2 Peter refers to Paul's "letters" and "the other Scriptures."

In the biblical collection of books there are, in turn, books which present themselves as further collections of texts from various authors, for instance Psalms or the proverbs gathered from the surrounding region (Proverbs). The fact that many of the books otherwise often consisted of different pre-existing parts from various sources is not something that was first articulated by modern biblical research. Rather, it can be directly ascertained from the particulars of the books themselves or at least surmised.

According to the Christian tally, the Old Testament is a collection of 39 books. In the Christian tradition they are sorted as follows: five books of the laws of Moses (the Tora); twelve history books; five books counted as poetic or wisdom literature; five books of the Major Prophets; and 12 books of the Minor Prophets. Jews sort the same books somewhat differently and break them down to 24 books. In contrast to the Jews and Protestants, the Catholic Church has an additional seven books in the Old Testament, composed not in Hebrew but in Greek. They stem from the time between the Old Testament and the New Testament. The additional books are referred to as the "Apocrypha" (Catholics and Orthodox refer to them as "Deuterocanonical Books"). However, they are not counted as part of the Bible since they follow the Jewish canon (from around 135 A.D.) which did not include them.[8]

After Jesus' ministry upon the earth, in addition to the Old Testament there were more and more new documents from the Apostles, their fellow workers and other authors who in part are unknown, as in the case of the Letter to the Hebrews. In the end the New Testament stood as a collection of 27 documents grouped according to various criteria. Five documents are historical reports (four Gospels and the Book of Acts), 21 documents are teaching letters and letters of correction from the Apostles and their co-workers, and the last book is a prophetic-apocalyptic book.

The composition of the New Testament canon took place in stages. This means that at the time of the Apostles there were already certain compilations, for instance Paul's letters, which were in existence. However, it only gradually became apparent which of the documents would endure over time. From the beginning, Christians have not described the New Testament differently.

Holy and Perfect Language or Functional Language?

*The entire **Koran** is written in the same Koran-Arabic, which is regarded as a holy language and as the expression of highest perfection. For this reason the required daily prayers and the confession of faith may only be spoken in this form of Arabic.*

The three languages used in the **Bible**, Hebrew, Aramaic, and Greek, were in part used at times when they were in various stages of development, and each author brings his own flavor of the language to bear. They are use-based, every day languages, meaning for instance that the Aramaic

---

[8] See Thomas Schirrmacher, *Die Apokryphen*, Nürnberg: VTR, 2006.

words of Jesus are only available in a Greek translation. Additionally, every person can pray in any language in which he or she is conversant.

Ibn Rassoul writes the following about the **Koran**: "The words, style, and content of the Koran are detectably supernatural"[9] (e.g., Sura 71:1). I. A. Abu-Harb adds: "Since the Koran was revealed fourteen hundred years ago, no one has been in a position to compose a single chapter such as the chapters of the Koran as far as beauty, expressive language, majesty, wise law, true information, true prophecy, and other perfections are concerned."[10] What we designate as a "verse" in the Koran, the Koran itself refers to as an "ayat." That means a "miraculous sign" of God. Each verse of the Koran counts as its own miracle.

"Muslim theologians soon began to represent the view that the Koran, from a linguistic point of view, was perfect and unsurpassable. It is the most beautiful Arabic and exhibits unsurpassable harmony and perfection. The technical term for the Koran's unsurpassability, inimitableness, and uniqueness (Arabic i'jâz) has been used since the second half of the 9th century."[11] "One says: The language of the holy book is so completely unique that no other type of literature can even be compared with it, neither the language of the rhymed prose nor the unrhymed nor the manner of expression of the normal prose. The Koran explodes all literary categories with a character never before seen."[12]

Even if Arabic is not God's language and the holy language is actually only a specific Koran Arabic, Arabic is viewed by Islam to be the most perfect tool to reveal God's word. As a result of the fact that the Koran was recorded in Arabic, the language has received a key position within the entire Islamic world (Sura 12:2; 42:7).

Over against this the **Bible** does not lift up its language to the level of a norm. Which language would it be anyway? Churches throughout all time have assumed that the Bible was composed in completely normal, every day languages, and for that reason the study of the languages used therein helps to understand the Bible better.[13] To be sure, the Bible contains poetic

---

[9] Muhammad Ibn Rassoul, *Die ungefähre Bedeutung des Al-Qurán Al-Karim in deutscher Sprache*, Köln: Islamische Bibliothek, 2000^{23}, p. 564.
[10] I. A. Abu-Harb at www.islam-guide.com/de/frm-ch1-2.htm.
[11] Christine Schirrmacher, *Islam*, 2003, Christine Schirrmacher, *Der Islam* (2 vols.), Holzgerlingen: Hänssler 2003^2, vol. 1, p. 110.
[12] Hermann Stieglecker, *Die Glaubenslehren des Islam*, Paderborn: Schöningh 1983^2, p.383, par. 680.
[13] For the sake of completeness it should be mentioned that the idea was occasionally held in 17th and 18th century Lutheran orthodoxy that the language of the Bible was unflawed and, for example, grammatically faultless. However, it was precise-

verse of international stature, for instance in the Book of Psalms, or well thought out dramaturgical works such as the Book of Job or the Book of Esther. However, there are also ancestral records and administrative documents, which one normally does not hold to be linguistically elegant.

There has always been the understanding that there are different styles to be found among the biblical authors. One has, in part, very linguistically accomplished authors, for example demonstrated in the Psalms or Paul's letters, and, in part, authors with only a simple command of language, such as the Prophet Amos (who was a shepherd) or Peter (who was a fisherman).

Christian churches have always been aware of the fact that Jesus originally spoke Aramaic and that his words were handed down to readers and hearers in the world's commercial language, Greek. This has never been a problem for Christian churches. Grammatical errors in the New Testament, which arise for instance in Paul's long sentences (e.g., Ephesians 1:4-14), have also never been viewed as a problem. In spite of this, everyone understood what the authors, such as Paul, wanted to say.

Is Holy Language Effectual if not Understood, or is Proclamation Required in Order to Lead to Better Understanding?

*Reciting the **Koran** is an act of divine service, even if it is not understood. Reading out (recitation) and using the original Arabic text is of greater importance that understanding the text.*

As far as the text of the **Bible** is concerned, it is of integral importance that it be understood. For that reason the Bible has always been proclaimed by interpreting it, and its message has always been formulated anew so that every person understands what the message is.

What was just said about the **Koran** and its Arabic being unsurpassable applies only to the classical Arabic of the 6th century and not to the many variations of modern Arabic, whose speakers normally do not understand classical Arabic. This situation is likened to a modern Greek who cannot simply read the original text of the New Testament. For this reason there are millions of Muslims who say their prayers in this holy language without understanding what they are praying. Of course, it is often the case that they have been taught what the contents of the prayers are. Many Muslims

---

ly the pietists such as Johann Georg Hamann who refuted the idea. Even modern Christian fundamentalism recognizes grammatical mistakes by biblical authors.

memorize all of the Koran and can recite it in its entirety (comp. Sura 73:3,20; 75:17-18), without, however, understanding Arabic.[14] The office of Koran reciter is one of the most important Islamic offices, since many reciters have this activity as their primary occupation (Sura 75:17). There are actually several training centers that instruct reciters.

The practice of Islam requires at least a basic awareness of Arabic, since in Islam divine service only takes place in fully valid form in Koran Arabic. This means that above all that one should be able to pronounce Arabic, not that one necessarily understand it, even if it is better if one can understand.

The majority of Muslims nowadays are not of Arabic descent. Arabs account for a minority among the total. Their great influence has to do with the fact that Arabic is the language of the Koran (and Mecca lies in the Arab world). Influential Islamic theologians are in large part of Arab descent. Arab institutes of learning such as Cairo's al-Azhar-University belong to the list of the most important training centers. Arabic is the preferred language of commentaries on the Koran and of the standard theological and legal works. For many centuries written records (Hadithe) were only obtainable in Arabic.

The **Bible** does not have the notion of a holy language. The Revelation of John as well as the Book of Daniel prophesies that at one point, from all "tribes," God will be praised before his throne in all "tongues and languages" (Revelation 5:9-10; 7:9; 10:11; 11:9; 13:7; 14:6; 17:15; Daniel 7:14). "In contrast, the Bible speaks from the beginning of a world of peoples, of all nations, of all languages, who – as the Book of Revelation reports – will worship before God's throne in all languages (all tongues) at the end of time. They will come from all nations and from all tribes. From beginning to end the Bible has a view to a world of different peoples in its sight."[15]

Even in the Hebrew Old Testament there are Aramaic texts. The Old Testament already reports that words changed their meaning over the course of the centuries (e.g., 1 Samuel 9:9 with regard to the change in meaning from seer to prophet). Even if one wanted to view Hebrew as the holy language of the Jews, for the New Testament church it became clear at the latest with the miracles of Pentecost (Acts 2) that God by his Spirit

---

[14] Evidenced in Stieglecker, *Glaubenslehren*, 1982, p. 616 (par. 1122).
[15] Christine Schirrmacher, „Die Muslime und ihre Heilige Schrift – dargestellt an der Frage nach Frieden und Gewaltbereitschaft", Lecture in Leverkusen, 2003, p. 11 (.pdf file; for download see Bibliography).

intends to make his divine message understandable to everyone in his or her own mother language.

The Sunday sermon in Christian churches, as well as every form of proclaiming "God's word" in Christendom, is based on the notion that a Bible text which is read out needs an explanation to be truly understood. In the Old Testament it was also the case the holy texts were not only read aloud. Rather, the texts were interpreted in front of small groups (e.g., 2 Kings 23:2-4, Nehemiah 8:4-8). The earlier Lutheran and pietistic colloquialism that in a worship service one went "under the word," and the responsibility of the person preaching to proclaim "God's word" in each and every church, is not honored simply by the fact that a large number of longer Bible texts are used that are true to the original. It is rather the case that the message of the Bible should be made as relevant as possible and should speak understandably into the lives of the hearers.

Jesus and Paul also proclaimed the word of God by again and again proclaiming their subject matter in new formulations and not by reading aloud finished texts. Paul's address in front of the leading Greek philosophers in Athens (Acts 17:16-34) is an outstanding example for how one can proclaim Old and New Testament content to a completely different culture. To be sure, "God's word" means Jesus' words, but it can also constitute the respective Holy Scriptures that were in existence prior thereto (for instance the Old Testament in Mark 7:10-13; comp. John 10:34-35; Proverbs 30:5-6). It is not accidental that God's word is most often identified with the proclamation of the gospel (in the New Testament, for example, Acts 18:11; 1 Timothy 2:13; 2 Timothy 2:9; 1 Peter 4:11) and with the subject matter of the proclamation or the gospel itself (e.g., Acts 13:7; Romans 9:6; Ephesians 6:17; 1 Thessalonians 2:13; 1 John 2:14; Hebrews 13:7).

Can Translations be "God's Word?"

*The **Koran** is in principle unable to be translated; translations, as they have been permissible in recent times, constitute an approximate meaning and not God's word itself.*

The **Bible** itself demands translation as a way for its message to be understood. Additionally, for instance, the Bible translates the Aramaic words of Jesus into Greek. Bible translations are almost as old as the Bible itself. Bible translations count as "God's word" as does the original text.

The **Koran**, according to the unanimous opinion of Islamic scholars, is actually unable to be translated. A translation can only be an approximation.[16] For hundreds of years the Holy Koran could not be translated. It was not until the new onset of missionary and political activity in the 20th century that the Koran was translated by Muslims into many languages and disseminated. It should be noted hereby that every translation has only been viewed as an approximation of its meaning or a commentary on the Koran and not, however, as "God's word" itself. For this reason editions of the Koran that are translated by Muslims are called "commentaries," "approximations of the Koran," "the meaning of the Koran" or something similar. Abdoldjavad Falaturi writes: "Strictly speaking, the Koran is not translatable for Muslims. Translations present a helpful bridge to understanding."[17] I. A. Abu-Harb writes: "The Koran was revealed to Mohammed solely in Arabic, and any translation, be it in German or any other language, is neither the Koran nor a version of the Koran. Rather, it is the attempt at a translation of the meaning of the Koran. The Koran exists only in Arabic as it was revealed."[18]

Good translations of the **Bible** for readers and hearers were an integral part of the Jewish and Christian faiths, and the first translations of the Old Testament are over 2000 years old. The first translations of the New Testament come from the early days of Christianity. The Greek translation of the Old Testament, the Septuagint, as well as the Aramaic (Targumim) and the Syrian (Peschitta) versions played a major role in the pre-Christian period. The first multi-lingual editions of the New Testament stem from the 2nd century A.D.

For Christians is it understood that their Holy Scriptures can be translated into every language, and missionary activity does not consist in reading out their holy texts in the original languages. Reference has already been made to the proof of multilingualism of the Holy Spirit on Pentecost. And Paul sounds a warning against speaking a language in worship services that visitors do not understand. If this occurs, visitors could think that the Christians are "out of their minds." On the other hand, if they understand the message they might possibly begin to worship God (1 Corinthians 14:23-25).

---

[16] According to, e.g., Rassoul, *Bedeutung*, 2000, pp. 567-568; also comp. A. L. Tibawi, "Is the Qur'an translatable? Early Muslim opinion" in: Colin Turner, *The Koran: Critical Concepts in Islamic Studies*, London: Routledge Curzon, 2004, pp. 1-13.

[17] Abdoldjavad Falaturi in *WDR* (ed.), *Der Koran: Ein fremdes Heiligtum entdecken*, Köln: WDR, 1994, p.11.

[18] I. A. Abu-Harb at www.islam-guide.com/de/frm-ch3-7.htm.

In 1 Corinthians 9:19-23 Paul gives reasons for the necessity of adapting linguistically (and adapting in other ways) to other people. Christians are therefore not only responsible for stating the message of salvation by Jesus Christ. Rather, they are also responsible for making themselves understood. The Bible also testifies to the amazing fact of the necessity of being able to proclaim the gospel to each target group in a new and different way by presenting the life story of the founder of Christianity in quadruplicate.[19]

Literal or Actual Meaning? The Letter or the Spirit?

*The interpretation of the **Koran** does not have a distinction corresponding to this biblical differentiation.*

The **Bible** warns that literalness can cause the actual meaning to be lost.

The **Koran** is taken to have been written in perfect language and for that reason it is to be understood in its direct meaning. Naturally there is a substantial history of Koran exegetics. However, the idea that the message and the actual meaning could get lost if one is too oriented towards the text and too little towards the message is foreign to the Islamic view of the Koran.

In the **Bible** the devil is presented quite simply as the critic of the word of God. This does not prevent him from quoting the Bible and attempting to render it ineffective by misusing it. He prefers to quote God word for word. The devil does so in a manner that is literal but incorrect, as is the case in the temptation of Jesus (Matthew 4:7-7; Luke 4:11-13). A literal interpretation therefore does not guarantee that a person has correctly understood God's message. Jesus withstood Satan's literal interpretation by responding with the word of God (Matthew 4:7; Luke 4:13) in a form that he understood in a metaphorical and spiritual manner. The conclusions that Christians serve the "Spirit" and not the "letter" (Romans 7:6; 2 Corinthians 3:6-11), and that the letter can kill (2 Corinthians 3:6) are also warnings about excessive literalness. This is the case even if these warnings go farther to address neglecting the living Spirit, life and the actual message for the sake of only holding to correct externals.

---

[19] Comp. to target groups in Frank Koppelin, "The Gospels as Evidence . . .," 2005 (complete list of literature in Bibliography).

A Uniform and Holy Style or a Variety of Styles?

*According to the Muslim notion, the **Koran** is written in a single style of holy Koran Arabic.*

The **Bible** contains the entire spectrum of human literary modes of expression in various languages and reflects the linguistic development of various times. There is no specific style or language in which one says that God reveals himself; rather, God can principally use every variation of human means of expression for the proclamation of his message.

It was made clear in the prior section that the **Koran** is written in a single, inimitable style.

Outwardly the **Bible** is precisely the opposite. The literary diversity of the biblical books is enormous. Legal writings stand next to love songs, historical reports next to songs of lament, collections of proverbs next to family histories, royal documents next to collections of psalms, private letters next to official letters, extensive dialogs next to directions given to workers, apocalyptic warnings next to visions pictured in detail, autobiographical reminiscences next to irony, jokes, riddles and fables.[20]

This diverse manner of God's speaking in history through people is described by the New Testament as follows: "In the past God spoke to our forefathers through the prophets at many times and in various ways,[2] but in these last days he has spoken to us by his Son . . ." (Hebrews 1:1-2a). In the New Testament the diversity of God's manner of speaking continued after the revelation through the "Son," Jesus Christ. Be reminded again that the story of the life of Jesus in the New Testament is recounted four times, and in each of these different language styles are used.

Were the Authors Passive Recipients or were Their Personalities Actively Involved?

*The **Koran** emerged in a manner whereby Mohammed's personality was not active at the time of inspiration.*

The **Bible** emerged in a manner whereby there was active involvement on the part of the most diverse personalities who acted as authors. Even in cases where one was dealing with direct verbal expression or visions, the

---

[20] Comp. Thomas Schirrmacher, *Die Vielfalt biblischer Sprache: Über 100 alt- und neutestamentliche Stilarten, Ausdrucksweisen, Redeweisen und Gliederungsformen*, Bonn: VKW, 2001².

recipient remained active by, for instance, either inquiring or expressing desires.

The **Koran** and Islamic theology place great value on the fact that the Koran did not come from Mohammed and that Mohammed was a passive recipient when receiving revelation. He was unable to resist the revelation, and he was unable to influence its course. "He received the fragments of the Koran in the state of a mental trance, which even inundated his conscious and volitional personality at the point where it had to do with his own concerns and worries."[21] "It is not via the Koran but rather via reliable Hadithe that we experience something about the . . . ecstatic states which befell him . . .; an enveloping could at most (Sura 73:1; 74:1) contain a quiet hint about it."[22] "In a number of traditions it is reported how he fell to the ground when he had prophetic onsets, changed color and became red in his face as if he had the highest possible fever; large drops of sweat would cover his forehead even on the coldest winter days; he would hoarsely breathe in a way that reminded one of the snorting of a camel. He was attended to by being wrapped and a leather cushion was placed under his head. He himself would say that he sometimes heard a speaking voice, like one person speaking to another, and sometimes the sound somewhat like that of a bell that was particularly excruciating for him. These uncanny conditions, more than anything, else produced in his followers an unshakeable faith in the supernatural origin of his inspiration and speaks in favor of the truth of these portrayals."[23] "The symptoms of revelation were impressive. When Mohammed sensed that a revelation was nearing, he was overcome by shivers and he usually had a covering or a coat given to him ("O you who have wrapped up in your garments!", 73:1, "O you who are clothed!", 74:1), under which one could hear him groaning, snorting, and screaming. After the revelation he was covered in sweat and suffered from headaches, which he had treated with compresses . . . After the ceremonious announcement of the pilgrimage of departure, when the prophet sat on a camel, the force of a verse coming down threw the animal to its knees."[24]

Such summaries from the Koran and related traditions are not viewed critically by Muslims. Rather, they are viewed as evidence for the fact that Mohammed received revelation and did not produce it himself. Additional-

---

[21] Emile Dermenghem, *Mohammed, in Selbstzeugnissen und Bilddokumenten dargestellt*, Reinbek, 1960¹, 1980². p. 34.
[22] Enzyklopädie des Islam. vol. II. Brill: 1927. p. 1140.
[23] Frants Buhl. *Das Leben Muhammeds*. Verlag von Quelle und Meyer: Leipzig, 1930. pp. 138-139. [23] Dermenghem, *Mohammed*. pp. 20-21.
[24] Dermenghem, *Mohammed*. pp. 20-21.

ly, the fact that Mohammed possibly could neither read nor write (Sura 62:2) is mostly invoked to show that it was impossible for him to have either brought about the Koran texts himself or to have, for instance, derived them in part from reading the Bible.

When the **Bible** is described as inspired by the Spirit of God (2 Timothy 3:16) or is called "God's word" (Mark 7:13), what is meant is that God used human authors in a marvelous way to say what he wanted to reveal to mankind. It is not that God was the author instead of people. Even in 2 Peter 1:21 it is said of the "prophecy" that it "never had its origin in the will of man" but that it means that "men spoke from God as they were carried along by the Holy Spirit."

Christian churches believed early on that the Holy Spirit brought about the fact that the entire Bible was consolidated into a final unity, not, however, in the sense that in some sort of a 'manipulated' edition all parts were stylistically or otherwise perfectly harmonized with each other. Rather, it is meant in the sense that the Bible is complementary and in its great diversity of voices conveys, by God's order, what mankind needs as God's word.

According to the Christian notion, God does not force his word to be composed nor does he shut off human personality, such as is the case in many mechanically inspired revelations in various religions, including some Christian sects. When God's Spirit acts on and in people, according to the Christian understanding, he makes them true personalities – generally in the life of faith as well as particularly by the revelation of his word. Even the Old Testament and New Testament prophets, who saw unbelievable images in ecstatic-like conditions, were able to converse sensibly with the angels who were interpreting the visions (e.g., in John's Revelation or in Daniel and Ezekiel). In 1 Corinthians 14:32 Paul considers it natural that prophets are in control of themselves and in control of the revelations that are given to them: "The spirits of prophets are subject to the control of prophets" (1 Corinthians 14:32). Paul does not hold it to be Christian to be able to be led astray by powers to false gods (1 Corinthians 12:2).

A loss of personality in the Bible is a sign of the work of the devil. God, in contrast, gives everything to humanity as a free agent and desires that the true personality rule itself (1 Timothy 3:2; Galatians 5:23) to soberly and calmly decide for God's way (comp. 1 Peter 5:2). In an extreme case the possessed Garasene (Matthew 8:28-34; Mark 5:1-20; Luke 8:26-39) makes that point clearly. Evil causes him to live like an animal such that all recognizable semblance of personality appears to be missing. Jesus' freeing word causes his personality to return so that he can again speak sensibly with Jesus. This is frightfully realized by the outsiders (Matthew 5:15; Luke 8:35).

A Divine Style or do the Authors have Numerous Styles?

*The **Koran** knows only God as the author and with this a single, divine style. Mohammed's style is found in his words that are handed down by tradition but not, however, in the Koran.*

In the **Bible** the most varied personalities appear as authors, and they exhibit their own style, their own point of view and often their own completely personal story with God. The Bible is completely and wholly man's word. And only as such, then, is it also, in an unsearchable interplay, fully and wholly God's word by the activity of the Holy Spirit.

The **Koran** and Islamic theology place a lot of value on the fact that the Koran does not stem from Mohammed and does not reflect his personality and his point of view (even when the Koran reports much about Mohammed as an envoy of God and imbues him with authority). Rather, the Koran is written in divine style.

According to its own view of itself, the **Bible** was not received by uninvolved parties or as a mechanical dictation. Rather, the contrary is the case. The Bible was written by true characters whose unmistakable differences are expressed in their writings. Inspiration, that is the overall working of the Holy Spirit, does not exclude human personality. In fact, it leads to the complete development of one's personality.

The human side of the Bible is not proof against the divine inspiration of the Bible. The thought that the Holy Scriptures are God's word because no person is involved or because the people involved are not capable of being active, is missing from the Bible as much as it is missing from the history of Christianity.

Christian teaching on the divine inspiration of the Scriptures was never understood to mean that God dictated in his own style to replaceable authors. Rather, it was always the case that the Spirit of God watched over what was finally handed down for all time. All the while the personalities of the biblical writers, their life stories, their education, and their style, all had their influence. In the Bible the highly educated and multilingual Paul stands unmistakably next to the simple fisherman Peter. Luke, the Greek who worked with history (Luke 1:1-4), composed a completely different gospel from the somewhat spiritualized Jew John, whose Greek writing was influenced by his Aramaic. And the Lamentations of the failed prophet

Jeremiah (at least he was not listened to) would not and could not have been written by the successful prophet Daniel. References to the four different gospels have already been made.

A Timeless Text or is History Central?

*Even if the **Koran** was written in a historical setting, it is basically eternal and above all calls for submission to the eternal creator and does not intend to report stories. Historical events play a subordinate role in the Koran, so that it barely contains historical statements which a person could scrutinize or challenge.*

The **Bible** is in numerous senses a history book. For one, large parts of the Bible report history, because God is a God who acts in history. Secondly, the authors or characters are often in the center and are closely woven together in the formulation of quite a number of biblical books. Thirdly, the revelation of the Bible is historically progressive. That means it is often important to know what texts come from which time. Earlier portions are at times superseded by others or even suspended at later times. Many Old Testament requirements are, for example, no longer binding, just as not everything that Jesus did before his crucifixion was afterwards raised to a behavioral norm.

That the **Koran** is in a certain sense timeless is derived naturally from the fact that the "original document," the "mother of the book," had eternally existed in Heaven. "The contents of the Koran, which Mohammed received to read, were not composed as a report of historical events. They are in a sense timeless and ahistorical. To be sure, there are commentaries on and instructions from situations in Mohammed's life. But these were already determined before Mohammed existed. Allah composed the book so that it would fit to Mohammed's life."[25]

This leads to the fact that the Koran, in its arrangement, is not historically oriented, and even when it reports past events, they are seldom supplied with concrete historical details. "History prior to Mohammed is hinted at, but it largely remains imprecise. The Koran contains no chronology and no information regarding the time prior to Mohammed's life. The Koran hints at many events, the fact, for example, that prophets such as Adam or Abraham appeared before Mohammed. However, the Koran does not say anything about the years when they lived or in which periods of time

---

[25] Ulrich Neuenhausen, „Das heilige Buch des Islam" in: *Bibel und Gemeinde* 102 (2002) 1, pp. 60-61.

they lived and preached ..."[26] (see, e.g., Noah in Sura 71:1, 21, 26 or Moses in 79:14).

In addition to this comes the fact that the Koran's 114 Suras are neither arranged in a historical order nor are their verses ordered historically. The Suras are in principle ordered according to length; only the introductory Sura 1 is an exception. Sura 2 has 286 verses, and Sura 114 has 3 verses. The individual Suras do not produce a self-contained narrative. Rather, they are put together from separate sequences according to how Mohammed once recited them and how they were collected. Only few narratives or topics are self-contained, for example the story of Joseph in Sura 12. Muslim as well as non-Muslim Koran scholars are in agreement that the longer Suras in particular were not revealed in a coherent manner. Rather, it is more probably the case that the longer Suras were compiled from many individual verses.

So it is that we encounter almost 20 Old and New Testament characters in the Koran, for example, Adam, Abraham, Moses, Job, David, John the Baptist, and, naturally, Jesus Christ. At times the reports in the Koran regarding their activities deviate in large part from those depicted in the Bible, because in the Koran these characters are all types for the sending of Mohammed. In these prophetic narratives there are practically no historical sequences of events or datings of the reports. As a rule there are also no self-contained prophetic narratives with a beginning and an end. Rather, there are only allusions to the prophets. "We are not dealing with historical reports here; knowledge of them is presupposed,"[27] writes Murad Hofmann.

No biography of Mohammed can be created from the Koran. In fact, what has been handed down (Hadithe) and the biographies of the early prophets are necessary. For this reason the Koran provides few pointers that could be considered for historical criticism if such criticism were admissible in Islam.

"The **Bible** reports God's history with people. It unfolds history progressively from the creation up to Revelation. The Bible also contains secular history and names concrete dates, numbers, names or ancestral registries. This data appears to us today to be of little significance. However, it expresses the fact that the Bible seeks to be a historical document."[28]

The written word of God is often simply the historical testimony of God's activity in history, for instance in the exodus from Egypt, in the giv-

---

[26] Schirrmacher, „Die Muslime und ihre Heilige Schrift," p. 9.
[27] Murad Hofmann (ed.), *Der Koran*, Kreuzlingen: Hugendubel, 2007, p.12.
[28] Schirrmacher, „Die Muslime und ihre Heilige Schrift," p. 9.

ing of the covenant on Sinai, in dedicating the temple as well as in Jesus' passion week or in the Apostolic Council. The Bible again and again makes itself dependent on the historical reality of the events it reports (e.g., with respect to the resurrection in 1 Corinthians 15:1-8, 14-20a).

This does not lift the Bible above historical truth and historical verifiability. Rather, it asserts the claim that a historical examination will demonstrate the truth of Scripture. Friend and foe alike are invited to conduct historical work, such that Paul for instance refers to the eye witnesses of the resurrection who are still alive (I Corinthians 15:15).

There is not a holy scripture that has its texts so anchored in the respective history of the authors, the surroundings, and the salvific situation as does the Bible. This means that the Scriptures themselves provide an immense fund of historical material and, with it, the starting points for criticism. More than any other religion's holy scripture, the Bible reports the historical development of aspects of its religion (e.g., Deuteronomy 31:22-26; Joshua 1:8; 24:26; Proverbs 1:1; 30:1; 31:1; Jeremiah 1:1-3; Luke 1:1-4; Revelation 1:9-11). It is no wonder that later biblical critical research was able to so easily study and criticize the history of the books of the Bible. For centuries, thousands of historical chronologies and geographic details in the Bible have presented material for archeological, historical, and cultural study.

Finally, the entire concept of the modern, western understanding of history is rooted in Judeo-Christian thought. For this reason, one is not able to place the Bible in opposition to historical scholarship.[29]

Timeless Validity or a Validity Found in the Development of the Plan of Salvation?

*The **Koran** assumes that all prophets at all time had the same message and that between the creation of man and the judgment a timeless and constant will of God exists.*

The **Bible** presupposes progressive revelation and assumes that with the development of the plan of salvation insight increases. It is also the case that earlier stages of revelation lapse.

In the **Koran** all prophets have the same task and message, as is also finally the case with Mohammed. Earlier documents such as the Torah, the Psalms and the Gospels principally had no other content and contained the

---

[29] Comp. John W. Montgomery, *Hat die Weltgeschichte einen Sinn? Geschichtsphilosophien auf dem Prüfstand*, Bonn: VKW, 2003².

same timeless claims as the Koran. For this reason, regardless of the command, when it was revealed or for which time it was revealed are not relevant questions.

In the **Bible** the plan of salvation plays a prominent role. The times prior to, during and after the Aaronite/Levite priesthood are clearly differentiated and vary also with respect to all aspects of worship. Abraham made sacrifices on an altar erected by himself. This was later followed by the tabernacle, which was a transportable sanctuary that accompanied the wanderings of the Israelites. Eventually it was positioned in Jerusalem. What followed were the first and second temples and ultimately, in the New Testament, the church of Jesus as an invisible temple and the physical destruction of the visible temple. All of these stages of development do not contradict each other. Rather, they belong organically together and are yet connected with many additional regulations and spiritual truths that also changed, respectively. They are not invalid in the sense that the Christian church can no longer draw any spiritual truths from them, but they in large part lapsed insofar as execution is concerned. Christians study the sacrifices of the Old Testament, classify them with respect to salvific history but do not perform such sacrifices today. Christians are unable to understand the crucifixion of Jesus without the Old Testament background, even though it was Jesus himself who overrode vast portions of the Old Testament.

When studying the Bible, it is always important to classify the events, regulations, and commands according to salvific history. Therefore, pre-critical theology was never able to completely get around considering the historical character of the Bible for the purposes of interpretation.

Political development can serve as an example. There are innumerable political systems running through the Bible. In the beginning of the Bible there were elders and tribal princes. These were followed by judges, a federal state with a council, kingship in various forms, and repeatedly foreign rule. In New Testament times Jesus assigned believers' loyalty vis-à-vis the Jewish state, which at times had been a loyalty to the states that had at times ruled over Israel (e.g., Joseph in Egypt, Daniel in Babylon), to the Roman state: "Give to Caesar what is Caesar's, and to God what is God's" (Matthew 22:21; Mark12:17; Luke 20:25). Paul also instructed Christians to obey the Roman state (Romans 13:17). For an understanding of biblical texts, it is always important to consider in which political structure and milieu something was stated.

Veneration of the Printed Copy or Use as a Basic Object of Utility?

*Copies of the **Koran** are venerated by Muslims and treated with particular regard. Treating the Koran with disregard is taken to be blasphemy.*

Copies of the **Bible** are objects of utility, which are often worn out by convinced Christians and contain various markings. Expensive copies of the Bible are valued more for their artistic, material, historical, or personal value.

In Islam the **Koran** is revered not only for its content. Rather, each individual copy of the Koran is revered, be it a written version from earlier times or today's printed version. A copy of the Koran is kissed as a sign of veneration and is treated with great care. It is wrapped in a towel and kept displayed in a special and elevated place. The Koran is never kept on the ground. A copy of the Koran is only to be taken into the hands after a ritual hand washing. In any event, it is never to be touched with unclean hands or in any other unclean state is it to be handled or kissed (e.g., during the time of menstruation). The Koran is not allowed to be dirtied, damaged, ripped, burned, or thrown away. What this means for the strict Muslim is that it is not possible to throw a newspaper with verses from the Koran into the recyclable paper bin. The Koran may not be taken to any location where uncleanliness cannot be avoided. Principally this even applies to every written Sura from the Koran and every object furnished with Suras. All of this is seen as blasphemy and in many Islamic countries is a severe offense and even considered as falling away from the faith. Such offences can often be punishable by imprisonment or even death.

The Koran has the power to bless (Arabic barak). This makes copies of the Koran, as well as individually written verses, fitting for giving blessing or, for example, for healing from sickness. Even though it does not correspond to official theology, verses from the Koran can be dipped in water which is then drunk or placed in leather pouches and worn as an amulet. "For this reason, a verse from the Koran which is on a vehicle, a picture, or something similar, has a different purpose from verses which Christians hang on the wall or memorize: verses from the Koran are supposed to protect, disperse power and have an effect."[30] ". . . Nothing is ever to be written in the Koran and verses are never to be marked. . . . Muslims are astonished when they see how 'casually' Christians treat the Bible."[31]

---

[30] Neuenhausen, „Das heilige Buch des Islam," p. 61.
[31] Op. cit, p. 59.

The 'casual' manner in which Christians treat the **Bible** is precisely the sign that a person lives with the Bible. The fact that the Bible is often studied is demonstrated by worn copies. A Bible that is no longer needed can therefore be disposed of unproblematically and replaced with a new one. The way one treats a copy of the Bible is not necessarily an indication of the relationship a person has with God.

Even in those situations where in Christian liturgy a copy of the Bible is particularly revered and for instance is kissed during the liturgy or held up or set out on display as an altar Bible, the reverence for the Bible has to do with the contents and not with the copy itself. Of course, in the history of Christian art there are absolutely beautiful copies of the Bible that have been produced, and there are many readers of the Bible who have obtained special editions. Still, that always serves to venerate the contents and not the special copy of the Bible.

Superiority or Self-Criticism?

*The **Koran** serves above all to substantiate and proclaim the supremacy of God, his revelation, his prophet Mohammed, and believers.*

Where the **Koran** is directed against people, it is not directed against believers but rather against others. Self-criticism would mean the supremacy of truth is called into question.

Above all the **Bible** intends to substantiate and proclaim God's mercy for a world living at enmity with him; it likewise intends to substantiate and proclaim God's mercy toward his people, insofar as they have turned from him. When the **Bible** directs itself against people, it does this above all against the Jews in the Old Testament and Christians in the New Testament. Unbelievers or pagans are even at times held before believers as role models. The Bible is not very useful when it comes to celebrating the condition of Christians or Jews. In fact, revelation very often directs itself critically against God's people and frequently calls the true situation relentlessly what it is.

The **Koran** differentiates between two types of people. There are those who submit to God with the prophets and for that reason will triumph in every aspect. And there are the unbelievers who do not submit to God and for that reason are doomed. Above all, the Koran intends to establish the preeminence of God, his prophet Mohammed, and believers. The "preemi-

I. The Bible and the Koran as "God's Word" ... 31

nence"[32] of the Koran and the "victory"[33] of Islam (Sura 110:1) is not taken to be an offensive matter, but rather an inevitable consequence of the truth.

Islam does not seek to discourage believers via self-criticism and obscure the crystal clear truth. This plays a role in the understanding of sin, as we will see, because people are at all times considered to be basically capable of doing good.

The **Bible** is full of critical accounts about the people of God. The Old Testament vehemently proclaims monotheism, but it also relentlessly reveals how difficult it was to achieve this among the Jews. David's adultery and murder do not weaken the Psalms. Rather, they provide the occasion for the most important psalm of repentance in the Old Testament and in the history of the church (Psalm 51, with reference to 2 Samuel 6-7). Not only David, but also Moses and Paul, were murderers. It is not from writings which oppose the Scriptures that we find out about Peter's failings, including his idea that Jesus' sufferings were senseless, his statement shortly before the crucifixion in which he guaranteed to never deny Jesus (Matthew 26:33-35), and the incident whereby he had to be sharply criticized by the Apostle Paul. Rather, we find out about the sins of biblical characters in the Bible itself. The New Testament reports both that the early church commenced developing a social program very early (Acts 6) and that the wealthy members of the church often let the poor in the church go hungry (1 Corinthians 11:21-22), as well as the fact that they did not pay wages on time (James 5:4). Complete books of the Old Testament are dedicated to ruthlessly revealing the conditions among the Jews (e.g., the Prophet Micah), and complete books of the New Testament expose the upsetting situation in Christian churches (e.g., 1 Corinthians).

It is neither the pagan peoples in the Old Testament nor the Romans and the Greeks in the New Testament whose atrocities and misguided notions are central. Rather, it is the errors of the alleged or actual people of God. In the church in Corinth Paul discovered a form of incest which is "of a kind that does not occur even among pagans" (1 Corinthians 1:1b). All too often God has to call on an outsider in order to bring his people back to their senses.

In no religion do the followers get such a bad report as in the Old and New Testaments. The teaching that Jews and Christians are sinners and are capable of the worst acts is graphically shown in the Bible. Paul writes to Christians the following: "So, if you think you are standing firm, be careful

---

[32] Title of the chapter regarding the meaning of the Koran in Azzedine Guellouz's *Der Koran*, Bergisch Gladbach: Bastei-Lübbe, 1998, p.77.
[33] See the many evidences in the Koran presented in Hofmann, *Koran*, p. 511.

that you don't fall!" (1 Corinthians 10:12). He admonishes them in view of judging the Jews, exhorting them to not think of themselves as something better: "Do not be arrogant, but be afraid" (Romans 11:18-22).

Self-criticism belongs to the essence of being a Christian. To become a Christian means namely to first see oneself as a sinner, and not to identify the sins of others. Christians are not better. They only 'have it better.' According to Luther, being a Christian means that one beggar tells another where there is something to eat. Paul writes for instance: "For I am the least of the apostles and do not even deserve to be called an apostle, because I persecuted the church of God. But by the grace of God I am what I am . . ." (1 Corinthians 15:9-10a).

Within its own Holy Scriptures, Christianity takes note of a relentless and honest self-analysis. That has shaped the history of Christianity. Christian historians, not Muslim historians, have worked through the Crusades, and no religion has admitted its errors so clearly as Christianity in its thousands of years of history. It is no coincidence that critical historiography arose in the Christian Occident and was able to unfold against the churches.

Self-criticism is deeply rooted in the center of the Christian message – the good news of forgiveness. In the first chapters of the Bible it is reported that a consequence of turning away from God in the fall of man was that men began to look for guilt in others (Genesis 3:11-13). Since then people repeatedly shift the blame and guilt to others for all sorts of things, in the private sphere as well as in the high echelons of politics. Even if true searching for causes has its justification, Christianity does not mean that one looks for guilt in others. Rather, Christianity means that one first looks at himself. Jesus condemns the words of the Pharisee: "God, I thank you that I am not like other men . . ." and praises the words of the tax collector: "God, have mercy on me, a sinner" (Luke 18: 10-14). In the Bible faith begins with the recognition of one's own shortcomings.

A Jewish author writes: "In contrast to the Holy Scriptures of Mohammed, the Hebrew Bible is not a book but rather a library. It is a colorful tapestry of accounts which an entire people wove together over millennia. No misdeed on the part of the children of Israel is left out of this incomparable convolution. No wrongdoing by its greatest king is concealed. Paul Badde comments that 'up to the New Testament one can look at each book of the Bible as an objection, contradiction or a critical commentary of its own earlier history.' The result of this historical frankness is that since that time self-criticism in the Judeo-Christian world has counted as a virtue: it is a sign of strength and not an admission of weakness. In Islam it is different: a critique of one's own history? Unthinkable, a blasphemy! It would pull the foundation out from under revelation. It would be an insult to the prophet. Therefore, it is the case that up until today in countries shaped by Islam there is neither freedom of speech nor debate in freely elected parliaments."[34]

This self-criticism demands that one point out that Christianity did not live up to this demand for self-criticism often enough and that a wrong politico-religious feeling of superiority and an all too worldly conquering mentality were displayed. But still, one has to also see that Christianity did not work out the mistakes in its history by chance. A critical stance towards church history was not an invention of Christianity's detractors. Rather, it was something that Christianity itself had always practiced.

Faith: Submission or Trust with Lament and Doubt?

*In the **Koran** doubts and laments before God and his revelation are excluded and are understood as a direct attack on God.*

In the **Bible** there are complete books containing doubts and laments that are included (e.g., Lamentations, Jeremiah, the Psalms of lament). The Bible encourages a person to turn to God with laments and doubts, to suffer through them, and to overcome them in relationship with him.

The **Koran** is not familiar with, and does not contain, any laments directed towards God. It considers doubts about God and doubts about basic Islamic teachings as unacceptable and assumes that they do not arise in true believers. For a Muslim, laments and doubts can never be part of a conversation with God, because that would call God's dignity and position as creator and lord into question. To question God's goodness and his mercy for even a short time would be a demonstration of ingratitude and unbelief on the part of the person. Mankind is not entitled to accuse the omnipotent creator and lord of the world, to call him to account, or to question his actions, even in the case where it only has to do with a discussion.

Since mankind always remains God's servant and submissive subject, the sole stance to which he is entitled is that of humbly accepting the will of God in revelation and in actual history. "As a consequence of this belief, it is unthinkable for the Koran that a believing person would turn to God with laments or with accusations, as is the case in biblical testimonies. . . . The Koran forbids that people who are so moved by their own needs that they call God to account: "He cannot be questioned concerning what He

---

[34] Hannes Stein, *Moses und die Offenbarung der Demokratie*, Berlin: Rowohlt Berlin Verlag, 1998, p. 47.

does and they shall be questioned (Sura 21:22/23). There is no room here for voices of consternation about the disorder in the world and the suffering of the righteous, least of all the theodicy problem of how God allows certain things to happen or even brings them about. Unshaken, such appeals face the claim that everything created is absolutely perfect: '... you see no incongruity in the creation of the Beneficent God; then look again, can you see any disorder? Then turn back the eye again and again; your look shall come back to you confused while it is fatigued (Sura 67:3b-4)."[35]

In the **Bible** doubts and laments are often made into central themes and are a normal component of a living relationship with God, so much so that the Bible often has to with overcoming those very laments and doubts and regaining trust. Complete books are dedicated to this topic. Jeremiah's lamentations (Lamentations 1-5; Jeremiah 11-20) do not show a prophet who triumphs over evil. Rather it shows a struggling person has his deepest experiences with God through his doubts. The same applies to the prophet Elijah's depression. The Psalms of Lament have been a shaping factor in Judaism and for Christianity up to the present time (e.g., Psalms 3, 5, 6, 13, 44, 74, 77, and 79). In Job, God is not glibly proclaimed as the highest and most beautiful. Rather, after endless dialogues he remains the Creator and friend to whom one can also hold fast during suffering and confusion.

"The agitated Prophet Jeremiah counters somewhat challengingly: 'You are always righteous, O Lord, when I bring a case before you. Yet I would speak with you about your justice: Why does the way of the wicked prosper? Why do all the faithless live at ease? ... How long will the land lie parched and the grass in every field be withered?' (Jeremiah 12: 1, 4a). And the Psalmist calls to God in a manner that alternates between energetic imperatives and insistent questioning: 'Awake, O Lord! Why do you sleep? Rouse yourself! Do not reject us forever. Why do you hide your face and forget our misery and oppression? ... Rise up and help us; redeem us because of your unfailing love' (Psalm 44: 23-26)."[36]

Scholarly Treatment: Is it There to Defend the Scriptures or to Better Understand Them?

*In order to interpret the **Koran**, there is neither a hermeneutic nor specific linguistic principles. If something is written, then it is in a special form that*

---

[35] Zirker, *Koran*, p. 165.
[36] Ibid.

is not valid for any other text. "Scholarly literature relating to the Koran means literature that presents the Koran as the highest form of scholarship. It defends the Koran or has to do with correctly reciting the Koran."[37]

For the interpretation of the **Bible,** as for other texts, there are hermeneutical and linguistic principles that apply. Scholarly literature relating to the Bible means, therefore, writings that comment on and investigate the meaning, history and environment of the Bible and thereby help to better understand it or correctly apply it in our day. Such "scholarly literature" also questions the interpretations of earlier times and grapples with their claims.

The **Koran** is not a human text which can be investigated like every other text. Not only are the contents of the Koran perfect. The text itself is also perfect (Sura 10:1). There is indeed a long history of Koran exegesis. Particularly with the aid of "tradition" (Hadith), or the collected words and acts of Mohammed and his companions, Koran exegesis discusses the meaning of the text of the Koran. In this connection non-Islamic sources and the results of such linguistic and literary scholarship are not of importance.

Ulrich Neuenhausen writes critically from a Christian standpoint: "Whoever wants to discover a human style in the Koran is already considered an 'unbeliever.' It is therefore not astonishing that Islamic scholars, even if they approach the text of the Koran in a rational and critical manner, are excluded from the believing Muslim community. Whoever asks a Muslim for 'scholarly' literature about the Koran almost always receives 'apologetic' literature, namely books by convinced Muslims who prior to any investigation of the Koran have undertaken a defense of the faith."[38]

Nothing in the **Bible** hints at the idea that a better understanding of the Bible can not be promoted by anything that can otherwise help to understand human language. The inspiration of Scripture and the emphasis that a person needs the Holy Spirit in order to truly and spiritually understand the Scriptures (2 Peter 1:19-21) have also never been understood to mean that extra-biblical or non-Christian knowledge could not be employed in order to investigate the Bible. Furthermore, it has never been maintained that one has to cover one's eyes in the light of any facts when investigating the Bible.

---

[37] See, e.g., http://islamische-datenbank.de/Quranwissenschaft: Here Quranic science is equated with Tadschwid science, which addresses the question of how one should recite the Koran.

[38] Neuenhausen, „Das heilige Buch des Islam," p. 59.

Very early on the Bible was translated into many other languages. This fact has always had a particular meaning for interacting with the Bible. The Church Fathers of the first centuries zealously spotted different types of literature in the Bible (e.g., the parables of Jesus or the imprecatory Psalms) and discussed their correct interpretation.

The scholarly handling of the Scriptures is built upon the role of reason in Scriptures, reason, which indeed should remain subordinate to God, Christ and revelation (2 Corinthians 10:4-5; Psalm 111:10). At the same time scholarship is a tool used to decipher human language and communication and therefore to understand the Scriptures.[39] The Holy Spirit makes use of language and rationality in order to communicate his revelation and to make it understandable (1 Corinthians 14:15, 19). For this reason an understanding of the Scriptures that is true to the Bible contradicts neither a well thought out hermeneutic[40] nor a reasonable self-consciousness and questioning of one's own interpretive rules. Rather, it virtually presupposes these things. The interpretations of the past are repeatedly put to the test.

Textual Criticism – Yes or No?

*Textual Criticism of the **Koran** (that is to say a classification and evaluation of the original handwritten documents) is not foreseen, because of the uniformity of the tradition which has been handed down.*

Textual criticism of the **Bible** is always admissible and was practiced very early on by the Church Fathers, Reformers and Pietists. There has always been textually critical output in variant readings.

The fact that the **Koran** was not present as a complete text at the time of Mohammed's death (632 A.D.) is not disputed by Muslims. The individual parts were apparently brought together from notes, stones, palm stems, and from the hearts of men. In this sense there was a type of written early form of today's Koran. However, there was not a complete collection. It is the opinion of most Muslim theologians that the third Kalif Uth-

---

[39] Comp. Thomas Schirrmacher, *Ethik für Führungskräfte*, Gießen: Brunnen, 2002; also, *Wie erkenne ich den Willen Gottes?* Hamburg: RVB, 2001 (same as *Ethik*, 7 vols., VTR: Nürnberg, 2002³, vol. 3, pp. 353-388); Otto Weber, *Grundlagen der Dogmatik*. vol. 1. Neukirchener Verlag: Neukirchen, 1987⁷ (1955¹), pp. 214-218.

[40] For example Kinker, *Bibel*, 2003; Ramm, *Hermeneutik*, 1998; Jakob van Bruggen. *Wie lesen wir die Bibel?* Hänssler: Neuhausen, 1998 [for more details see Bibliography]; Walter C. Kaiser/Moisés Silva, *An Introduction to Biblical Hermeneutics*, Zondervan: Grand Rapids, 1994; Milton S. Terry, *Biblical Hermeneutics*. Zondervan: Grand Rapids, 1984¹² (English original version 1890¹).

man (644-656 A.D.) collected all versions and checked the authority of the individual sections, whereupon the edition of the Koran he produced around 650 A.D. was made binding for everyone. Likewise, there are numerous problems of textual criticism that Islamic theology has always intensively discussed, including the "abrogation" of already existing, revealed verses of the Koran which were extinguished by God. That still does not change the idea that textual criticism as such is not admissible. Rather, the text that is available at the present is considered to be consistent and unaltered. There are no editions of the Koran that reflect textual criticism, or that compare different written records, be they from Muslims or from other researchers.

The history of the **Bible** has always simultaneously been time a history of textual criticism. Long before textual criticism became a part of the modern historical critical method, men who highly esteemed the inspiration of the Bible, including most of the distinguished Church Fathers and many reformers, conducted comprehensive textually critical studies. Most of the people publishing editions reflecting textual criticism, which compare the numerous handwritten documents with each other, belong to that group of people to whom we would today refer to as "Bible-believing," including Erasmus of Rotterdam, Calvin's successor Theodore Beza or the leading Pietist Johann Albrecht Bengel. In short, since the Bible always was also considered a human book, it was perennially assumed that in light of the repeated copying of the texts, the Bible was subject to the normal principles of human transmission. Furthermore, this meant that there was no other Bible than the one that was composed from many reliable manuscripts.

Comparison of the Understandings of Biblical and Koranic Inspiration	
Bible	**Koran**
A. God and Man or only God?	
God and man are both authors (complementarity with each contributing 100%).	Only God is the author (100% divine, 0% human).
The Bible emerged successively over the course of a long period of history; the individual books appeared successively as people wrote them down and arranged them.	The Koran was not written. Rather, it was "sent down" and had always been with God, complete in heaven as original manuscript ("mother of the book").

Numerous and diverse authors.	No human author, only a human recipient.
Reflects the human personality of the respective authors.	Has nothing to do with any particular human personality.
The texts are mostly closely tied to the life stories of their composers or to the people presented.	The Koran does not stand in any relation to the life story of Mohammed.
B. Various and Normal Forms of Language or a Uniform, Holy Language?	
Collection of 66 documents.	A uniform book.
Large amount of literary variety.	A uniform style.
No perfection found in the language; rather, "normal" language is utilized; grammatical "errors" are a matter of course; many styles of language and linguistic idiosyncrasies are present.	Perfection in the language is taken to be a sign of the miraculous character of the Koran.
Does not contain holy language, utilizes numerous, normal languages and language styles; important statements have only been preserved in translation (e.g., the words of Jesus).	Holy and perfect language.
Prayers are possible in every language on earth.	Around the world, the daily required prayers and the confession of faith are only acceptable before God in the language of the Koran.
Reading the Bible aloud in the original languages is senseless if the readers and the hearers do not understand these languages.	Reading the Koran aloud (reciting) in Arabic is required and commendable, even when the readers and the hearers do not understand Classical Arabic.
It is necessary to have the Bible translated and proclaimed in order to be understood; the message achieves its own effects.	Truth and effects are not dependent on understanding.

I. The Bible and the Koran as "God's Word" ...

C. Scholarly Treatment or Pure Defense?	
There is a responsibility to translate the Bible and make it understood.	Translation is really not a possibility; translations of the Koran are interpretations.
Textual criticism is admissible and is a part of history.	Textual criticism is not admissible.
Texts reflecting textual criticism in various versions have been available since very early on.	The doctrine of tradition assumes uniformity.
With respect to interpretation, the Bible is subject to hermeneutic and linguistic principles as are all other texts.	There is neither a hermeneutic nor a form of linguistic studies applicable to the interpretation of the Koran; and if so, then only insofar as there is a special form that does not apply to any other text.
"Scholarly" literature relating to the Bible means literature which for others is reasonably comprehensible and comments on and explores the meaning, history, and environment of the Bible.	"Scholarly" literature relating to the Koran refers to literature which presents and defends the Koran as the highest achievement of scholarship.
D. A Historical Book or an Ahistorical Book?	
Emerged over the course of centuries.	Was sent down in 22 years and was prior thereto always present in heaven.
Set down in writing in various cultures.	Revealed in a single culture.
Set down in writing and compiled in a large variety of geographic locations.	Revealed in a limited geographic region.
There are many details about the historical development of the Bible that are found in the Bible itself.	There are no historical details about the Koran's own development, particularly since it had no historical development.
Contains many historical, chronological and geographical details: fre-	Contains scant concrete historical details.

quent connections are made to the histories of other people.	
For different and ultimately all peoples.	Is in the first instance for the Arabic world.
Progressive revelation and progressive salvation narrative are central.	All prophets proclaim the eternally identical message.
No particular value is placed on an individual copy of the Bible.	Utmost respect and reverence is shown toward each individual copy.

E. Doubts, Laments, Trust or Simply Regarded as Correct?

Doubts and laments vis-à-vis God were recorded in the Word of God (e.g., Lamentations, imprecatory Psalms).	Doubts and laments vis-à-vis God are excluded and are not to be found in the Koran.
In the Bible there is a call to test God.	It is forbidden to scrutinize God, since it would be tantamount to calling the creator to account.
Faith means accepting things as true and trusting in God, trusting particularly in his propitiation.	Faith means accepting things as true and submitting to God.
God commits himself by oath. He enters into a covenant with mankind. He commits himself to his word.	God is not bound to his word. Rather, he is sovereign over it and inscrutable concerning it.
There is certainty in faith and salvation, since God commits himself to hold to his promise of salvation.	There is no final certainty, since God remains sovereign and in the end is completely free to decide differently.

F. Does God Reveal Himself or Remain Hidden?

God's word is considered to be a true revelation of the essence of God.	God reveals himself and yet remains hidden in spite of sending down the Koran.
God reveals himself in biblical revelation and even more in his Son Jesus Christ. It is Jesus Christ to whom biblical revelation points and who reveals God as a person.	God remains hidden and only sends down a book.
Jesus Christ is the incarnate word of God, by which the actual revelation	There is no revelation of God in per-

of God occurs in person.	son.
There are many Christian celebrations which refer to Jesus Christ. There are, however, no celebrations for the Bible.	The month of fasting, Ramadan, celebrates the sending down of the Koran. It ends with the celebration of breaking fast and culminates with the "Night of Power," commemorating the time of the first revelation to Mohammed.
The founder Jesus is above the Holy Scriptures. They receive their meaning from him. Jesus is the actual "word of God." The Scriptures, as "God's word," bear witness to him.	The religious founder Mohammed comes under the Holy Scriptures. He receives his meaning from the Scriptures, since he receives them.
The founder is not only a prophet. Rather, he is God himself and the one who brings and effects salvation.	The founder is only a prophet.
Above all God sent down Jesus from eternity. The book (the Bible) only announces this, testifies to it, and proclaims it.	God, exalted over all, sent down the Koran from eternity.
G. Self-Criticism or Triumph?	
There is a distinction between the letter and the spirit, i.e., between dead and formal implementation and living fulfillment with meaning and a message.	There is no comparable distinction between the letter and the spirit. The letter is the spirit.
A critical presentation of believers who "fail." In contrast, there is less room given to criticism of others, and unbelievers are able to be shown as role models.	There is a triumph of believers; there is no critical presentation of believers. In contrast, the critique of others takes up much space; unbelievers can never be role models.
There is a continual self-critique of believers in the Bible itself.	There is no self-critique of believers in the Koran.
There is a command to critique and scrutinize one's own religion.	There is prevention of, or a command with punishment attached, regarding all self-critique and scrutinization of one's own religion.

II. A Relationship With God and How it Emerges Through His Word

Has God Revealed Himself?

*Even if the revelation of God in the **Koran** comes from God, since the eternal Creator remains hidden even for his creatures, it is not a revelation of God himself and of his nature.*

The **Bible** has first and foremost the goal of revealing God and his nature and of establishing a relationship of trust towards him. Since this is the ultimate goal of revelation, it is no accident that the Bible views God's revelation of himself in the incarnation of the Son of God Jesus Christ as its own confirmation and excellence.

"In the **Koran** and in Islam God does not actually reveal himself at all. Islamic theology teaches that God is a mystery. He is separated from the creation. 'A veil surrounds him' is the way philosophy has formulated it. He exists in a space to which mankind does not have access. Beginning with himself, mankind cannot establish any sort of connection to God. There is no bridge between the Creator and creatures. God also does not send his revelation directly to mankind, but rather by the angel Gabriel. The tradition describes it as God speaking from behind a curtain, which mankind from his side cannot penetrate. He cannot recognize God. He cannot apprehend God, and he cannot understand him . . . God has thus never come out from behind his veil of seclusion. He has indeed conveyed a message. He sends mankind a sign (e.g., in his creation). The Koran is of the opinion that every person can recognize God in the creation. But he has not conveyed anything of himself or of his nature."[41]

In divine revelation, through the prophets and apostles, and above all in Jesus Christ, the **Bible** sees a true revelation of God's own self. God wants to come close to mankind, to establish peace and to reconcile with mankind, and to achieve a trusting relationship of mankind to God. According to the New Testament, mankind of himself is not able to recognize God the Father (John 1:18, 5:37, 6:46; Matthew 11:27; 1 Timothy 6:16; 1 John 4:12) and of himself knows nothing about God (Job 36:26). However, it is the God of love (2 Corinthians 13:1; 1 John 4:8,16) who sent himself as the first missionary to mankind (Genesis 3:9), then sent himself in the person

---

[41] Schirrmacher, „Die Muslime und ihre Heilige Schrift," p. 11.

of Jesus Christ (Matthew 10:40; Mark 9:37; Luke 10:16; Acts 3:20,26; John 3:17 and more often; comp. Isaiah 48:16), and then also came in the form of the Holy Spirit (John 14:26; 15:26; Luke 24:49) as the missionary par excellence to mankind. For this reason, Jesus says: "Anyone who has seen me has seen the Father" (John 14:9, similarly 12:45). In Jesus Christ, God lives among mankind (John 1:14). God "lives" in believers via the Holy Spirit (Romans 8:9), because God has "poured out his love into our hearts by the Holy Spirit, whom he has given us" (Romans 5:5b).

God
Christians and Muslims alike believe in God, the Creator of heaven and earth and the Creator of each individual person. He alone is omnipotent and has seen to it that his history with mankind as well as his will have been recorded in a book. At the end of time he will call all people to give a reckoning and to be judged by him.

Koran	Bible
1. **God** (*Allah*) is the Creator of the world and each individual person, but God is fully transcendent. This means that he is completely separated from the creation. There is no bridge between the Creator and creatures (Suras 55:1-78; 6:100-101).	1. **God** created man in his own image and as his counterpart. He reveals his nature in the creation and in his word. Jesus is the bridge between God and man, because in him God became man (John 1:14-15).
2. God has no children and there is nothing that is equal to him. Jesus is not God and may not be worshiped as God. The belief in the trinity is polytheism, which is the worst, unforgivable sin in Islam. This is due to the idea that polytheism is the "associating" of another essence with the almighty (Suras 5:72-73, 75; 4:171-172).	2. God's only Son is Jesus Christ. Jesus came as a person to earth and yet is himself God. Father, Son, and Holy Spirit are/is a single, triune God (John 1:1-2; Matthew 28:20). Next to him no other God is allowed to be worshiped (Exodus 20:1-3).
3. God is the Creator, but he is neither the father of the believers nor the father of Jesus Christ. The Koran accuses Christians of worshiping three Gods, namely God, Jesus, and	3. God is the Father of Jesus Christ. Whoever calls upon God by the Holy Spirit is his child (Romans 8:15-17). The Trinity consists of the Father, Son and the Holy Spirit (Mat-

Maria, and therefore of practicing polytheism (Sura 9:30-31).	thew 28:19). Mary is only a person and has no participation in the Trinity.
4. God has repeatedly spoken through prophets, who always proclaimed the same revelation from the one almighty God and announced the impending judgment (Sura 6:74-90).	4. The triune God, in the time prior to Jesus, revealed himself progressively and in manifold fashions as God and Lord. He spoke through many witnesses and prophets, and finally he spoke through his Son Jesus Christ (Hebrews 1:1-2; Hebrews 11).
5. God revealed himself in the Koran as the eternal, sole, almighty, omniscient, and merciful God, yet he did not reveal himself (Sura 7:156; 35:15).	5. The God of the Bible revealed himself as eternal, majestic, omniscient, and perfect, and he wants people to live in personal community with him and themselves be truth, life, light, and righteousness (Exodus 15:11; Psalm147:5; 1 John 4:7-9, 16).

Faith as Recognition of the Lordship of God, or Faith as a Mutual Relationship of Trust?

*In the **Koran**, faith (Arabic iman) expresses itself in the recognition of the sole, eternal God and his omnipotence and lordship. Faith is humble devotion to God and submission ("Islam") to his will. The latter means that man avoids what God views as evil and does what God calls good, thus to especially follow the five pillars of Islam.*

Central to the Bible is the conviction that "faith" (Hebrew emuna, Greek pistis, Latin fides) is a reaction to God's "faithfulness" and is a trust toward God and expression of a personal relationship toward God. This is the case even when for this relationship a recognition of certain doctrines of truth is included and it is assumed that the one who believes in God also wants to do his will. Trust in God is also specifically necessary due to the fact that the believer often does not do the will of God. Faith is thereby a mutual relationship of trust, because for God's "faithfulness" the same word is used.

Faith in the **Koran** and in Islam are above all the recognition of the lordship and omnipotence of God, that is to say, humble devotion to God and submission to his moral and historical will. Faith in God requires belief in the judgment, the angels, the Holy Scriptures and the prophets (Sura 2:177). Faith is not limited to a theoretical 'accepting something as true' with respect to certain truths. Rather, it has consequences, namely to do good and to avoid evil (Sura 3:110), to ". . . convey good news to those who believe and do good deeds . . ." (Sura 2:25), to follow the five pillars of Islam, to live this life responsibly before God, and in light of the knowledge of the sure coming of the future life to configure this one.

The Islamic confession of faith (Arabic shahada), which is the first of the five pillars of Islam, reads: "I testify that there is no god but God, and I testify that Mohammed is his prophet," whereby this is always said in Arabic.[42] With this the uniqueness of God (Arabic tauhid) of God is placed in the center, as well as the sending of Mohammed as the Prophet of God who announces this uniqueness. The confession is said several times daily in ritual prayer and plays a definitive role in the practice of faith for all men and women beyond puberty. A non-Muslim irreversibly crosses over to Islam by saying the confession in the presence of two witnesses or before an Iman or a Qadi.

In the **Bible** faith is a firm trust in God and an expression of a good personal relationship towards God. It is the same notion that identifies God's "faithfulness" towards mankind. Faith in the Old and New Testaments has both active and passive meanings. The former pertains to fidelity towards a person or a promise one has made; the latter is trust in the promises another makes. One can learn what faith is from the people of God throughout history who devoted their lives to God in unwavering trust and obedience (Hebrews 11).

As early as the time of the Old Testament it was visible that faith was not only a mere recognition of tenets or an external consent to a law. Rather, it is a deep and ultimate trust in the faithfulness and credibility of God and loving obedience to his will (Deuteronomy 32:20; Habakkuk 2:4). The New Testament rejects a mere 'accepting as true:' "You believe that there is one God. Good! Even the demons believe that – and shudder" (James 2:19).

In the New Testament the terms "belief" and "to believe" are used almost 500 times. The basic assertion of the New Testament consists in the fact that belief in God and belief in redemption as achieved by Jesus Christ

---

[42] Schiites add as praise for the fourth Khalif Ali (Nephew and son-in-law of Mohammed): "And Ali is the friend of God."

are necessary to obtain eternal life. The first Christians named themselves "believers" or "the believing" (Acts 2:44). In the letters of Paul, belief is set up against one's own works as a means of redemption (Romans 3:20-22). Belief is a gift of God, for which a person can ask and should ask, because in the final event it is impossible to acquire belief with one's own energy. It is for this reason that the believer prays: "I do believe; help me overcome my unbelief!" (Mark 9:24b).

According to the Bible, the good works of a person are of course a consequence of belief, and yet they are not the foundation of belief: "In the same way, faith by itself, if it is not accompanied by action, is dead" (James 2:17). The Bible also calls this "bearing fruit" ("If a man remains in me and I in him, he will bear much fruit . . ." John 15:5) and establishes this with the example of Jesus: "Whoever claims to live in him must walk as Jesus did" (1 John 2:6).

Is God Free from Obligation or Bound to His Promises?

*The **Koran** proclaims a God who is so absolute, sovereign, and independent that, in the final event, he never can, or wants to, commit himself with respect to people. Even with God's promises, there is always the qualification that he could decide differently and no one can prevent him, since he otherwise would be subject to man's judgment.*

The **Bible** proclaims a God who as Lord and Creator is absolute, sovereign, and independent. No one could resist him if he changed his plans and did not keep his promises. Neither man nor the creation could bind or force God. However, God binds himself to his own word and swears by himself. God is "faithful" and absolutely "trustworthy." His sovereignty comes precisely to bear in the fact that no one can prevent him from putting his plans, promises, and vows into action and holding to them.

In the **Koran** God is omnipotent and is for that reason always free and sovereign in his decisions. This also applies when he makes promises to mankind, because it is unthinkable that mankind could later make an accusation against God on the basis of such promises or think that he could dictate to God what he is to do. This applies especially to God's decision with respect to the Last Judgment. To be able to foretell here and now what will occur would presuppose being able to limit God's omnipotence and to stipulate his decision, which is not mankind's position. God is indeed identified as the gracious and merciful one, as the forgiving and magnanimous one, but with regard to forgiveness each believing Muslim will only have final assurance after death. "... But not (so) the Lord of the worlds; Who created me, then He has shown me the way ... And He who will cause me to die, then give me life; And who, I hope, will forgive me my mistakes on the day of judgment" (Sura 26:77-82).

The Koran identifies God at one point as cunning, whereby several Muslim commentators say this refers only to deception vis-à-vis unbelievers. Other commentators say that this has to do with everyone, since God cannot be limited nor nailed down. "He is the one who is best at devising tricks ..." (Sura 13:33) or translated otherwise, "He is full of treachery" (Rudi Paret). "And when those who disbelieved devised plans against you that they might confine you or slay you or drive you away; and they devised plans and Allah too had arranged a plan; and Allah is the best of planners," or otherwise translated "Allah schemes. He can do it best" (Sura 8:30). That is why the Koran indeed knows many vows, but it knows none in which God would obligate himself to mankind.43 Such a situation would place God and mankind on the same level.

In the **Bible** the most prominent characteristic of God is his reliability, trustworthiness, and truth (e.g., Exodus 34:6; Psalm 117:2). He is the "God of truth" (Isaiah 65:16), who is absolutely trustworthy. Whatever God has promised, "he is faithful in all he does (Psalm 33:4b). The "trust" ("belief") that relates to this "truthfulness" of God is not accidentally, along with "love," the most frequently used and most important description of the relationship between man and God. God has once and for all committed himself to save and redeem his creatures, and he has covenanted (Genesis 13:1-3; Exodus 20:1-3) to demonstrate his grace towards them and to save them from sin and death (Jonah 4:2). God confirmed the covenant of salvation with an indissolvable oath by his own name (Hebrews 5-6), "since there was no one greater for him to swear by" (Hebrews 6:13). It is no wonder that the signs of the covenant (sacraments), with which the beginning of the covenant (baptism) and the continual covenant renewal (Lord's Supper) in the "New Covenant" (1 Corinthians 11:25) are celebrated, are the external identifying features of the Christian church.

It is directly reported 82 times in the Bible that God swears by his own name (comp. Hebrews 6:13; Genesis 22:16; Exodus 32:13; Deuteronomy 32:40; Isaiah 45:23; Jeremiah 22:5, 44:26, 49:13; Amos 4:2, 6:8; Romans 14:11). Forty additional times he makes a covenant and provides mankind the steadfast assurance of his nature and action. An oath alone should not

---

[43] Also according to Lamya Kandil, „Schwüre in den mekkanischen Suren" in: Stefan Wild (ed.), *The Qur'an as Text*, Leiden: E. J. Brill, 1996, pp. 46-47; comp. pp. 51-57 regarding all vows in the Koran.

ground the truth, which for a God who never lies would be nonsensical. The unsworn message that Nineveh would be destroyed in 40 days (Jonah 3:4) was true, but it left open the possibility of a reversal. An oath makes a promise firm and irrevocable and underlines its irreversibility and ineradicability (Hebrews 6:16-18). If no one in the Old and New Testaments swears more frequently than the God of truth, then it is due to the fact that God thereby makes his promises irrevocable and binds himself with regard to the future.

A portrayal of God with two complementary sides is a distinct characteristic of the biblical revelation in Christianity and Judaism. On the one hand, God is absolutely sovereign; on the other hand, within the framework of a covenant with men, he binds himself and places obligations upon himself, whereby he allows himself to be evaluated. In this way, God graciously takes the initiative, so that his sovereign freedom leads to a trustworthy covenant with his people. This is clearly and classically seen at the beginning of the Ten Commandments: "I am the Lord your God, who brought you out of Egypt, out of the land of slavery. You shall . . ." (Exodus 20:2-3a). God first freed Israel, and then he called the people to abide. It was not the reverse.

The commitment that God places upon himself with an oath belongs to one of the core aspects of Christian belief. It is no accident that this absolute trustworthiness on the part of God also finds expression in the fact that he has given his revelation a final, written form. In it he commits himself with the gospel. It is all the less accidental that God outdoes himself by sending his Son Jesus Christ to become a man. The certainty that God reveals himself as a covenantal God, and as a God who freely commits himself in love – without mankind being able to force him – also demonstrates why in the Holy Scriptures particular promises and texts are repeatedly presented as completely credible (Psalm 119:43, 160; 2 Timothy 2:25; 1 Thessalonians 2:13; John 17:17).

A Prohibition Against Testing God or a Challenge to Test God?

*The **Koran** has no notion of God's trustworthiness being tested.*

In the **Bible** God himself repeatedly challenges believers to test his trustworthiness.

The **Koran** reports very often that God tests mankind (e.g., Sura 67:2) in order to see who holds to him. No creature is entitled to test the Creator or to call him to account. Again, God "cannot be questioned concerning what He does and they shall be questioned" (Sura 21:23).

In the **Bible** the emphasis on the trustworthiness of God always leads to a situation in which God not only tests people, but also to the reverse situation in which believers are called upon to test God (Malachi 3:10), to argue with him (Isaiah 1:18, 41:1, comp. also 45:9) and to assess whether he truly holds to his word. That God places commitments upon himself, that he reveals himself, and that he has given his word, are all things that can be applied to God. This means that God himself becomes the standard against which he can be measured.

If a believer does not understand God, he or she should not suppress the questions but rather discuss and experience the questions with God. God even calls an individual to this activity. In the end God indeed shows himself to be trustworthy, but not due to the fact that questions and probing are prohibited. Rather, it is due to the fact that he proves himself to be actually and really trustworthy according to the standards which he himself provides.

As we have just seen above, for this reason alone God allows himself to be intensely accused in lamentations and imprecatory Psalms when his promises are apparently not being kept. Repeatedly, the question arises of how there can be so much misery and suffering in the world where there is a good and loving God (e.g., Psalm 73; Job; Lamentations; Romans 9: 3, 5-6). However, suffering in a loveless and evil world is only a problem if one assumes that there is a standard for almighty God against which he can be judged, namely his own love and goodness. Paul can even ask: "Is God unjust?" (Romans 9:14). He indeed answers the question negatively (Romans 9:15-26), but it is typical that this question is raised and discussed in the Bible itself.

Is Love God's Reaction or is it the Deepest Indication of His Nature?

*In the **Koran** God's love means that God is graciously disposed towards believers who do his will. God loves those who love him.*

In the **Bible** God's love means that God pursues people who do not want to know anything about him, and he brings them home to him as their Father. God loves people so that they obey him.

One of the most basic statements of the **Koran** is that God is "the Merciful" (Sura 4:16). That becomes clear with the fact that all 144 Suras in the Koran (with the exception of Sura 9) begin with the introduction: "In

II. A Relationship With God and How it Emerges Through His Word

the name of Allah, the Beneficent, the Merciful." Occasionally there is mention of God's love, e.g., "Surely (as for) those who believe and do good deeds for them will Allah bring about love" (Sura 19:96). "The representatives of orthodoxy define mankind's love toward God as the readiness to obey him and to serve, a love of his ordinances, and of his favor and his reward. It is argued that love is a mutual affection such as that among friends or even between loved ones, and it includes equality between the loved and the loving. However, God's transcendence prevents thinking about such a relationship between God and mankind. Therefore, the assumption that between man and God such a loving friendship and intimacy can exist erroneously equates to an unbearable pretension from the side of people and a blasphemous vilification of God."[44]

In Islam, God's love may never be compared with human love. Here also God's greatness and omnipotence, his transcendence and complete otherness remain preserved so that a comparison to people or to interpersonal perceptions or characteristics would be unthinkable. In addition, in Islam God's love is an answer to mankind's obedience to him. "Say: if you love Allah, then follow me, Allah will love you and forgive you your faults, and Allah is forgiving, merciful" (Sura 3:31). The love of God does not constitute the center of the message of the Koran.[45] Rather, it is the confession of the uniqueness and oneness of God (Arabic tauhîd) as well as submission to his omnipotence and strength.

The statements of the **Bible**: "God is love" (1 John 4:8, 16) counts as a shining message of Christianity. God is not only one who gives love or acts lovingly. Rather, he is identical to love. He is "the God of love" (2 Corinthians 13:11b). His love towards his creatures is what moves God and is what is the motor for his actions in history, in particular for Israel's deliverance out of Egypt and other captivities and for sending his Son Jesus Christ: "For God so loved the world that he gave his one and only Son . . ." (John 3:16a). The Son of God who became man is ". . . how God showed his love among us . . ." (1 John 4:9a). Due to the fact that God himself is love, all love proceeds from God (1 John 4:7). All relationships among people and their relationship to God should be marked by love. Otherwise,

---

[44] Adel Theodor Khoury, *Der Koran Arabisch-Deutsch. Übersetzung und wissenschaftlicher Kommentar*. 12 vols., Gütersloh: Gütersloher Verlagshaus, 1990-2001, vol. 2, pp. 207-208.
[45] In contrast, in Islamic mysticism the love of God is emphasized, since the believer seeks to approach God and merge with God up to the point of having God indwell him. However, the believer seeks to love God without knowing in the final event whether God loves him.

they are in the end worthless. The greatest sacrifice and the most selfless act mean nothing before God if their motive is not love towards God and neighbor. Paul's "hymn to love" in 1 Corinthians 13 describes this emphatically: "If I speak in the tongues of men and of angels, but have not love, I am only a resounding gong or a clanging cymbal. If I have the gift of prophecy and can fathom all mysteries and all knowledge, and if I have a faith that can move mountains, but have not love, I am nothing. If I give all I possess to the poor and surrender my body to the flames, but have not love, I gain nothing" (1 Corinthians 13:1-3).

Since God, who is the source of all love, gives his love to mankind, man, for his part, is in a position to love God. This is the reason the following is said: "Love the Lord your God with all your heart and with all your soul and with all your strength" (Deuteronomy 6:5) as well as: ". . . love your neighbor as yourself" (Leviticus 19:18). Both these commandments are the commandments that Jesus himself repeatedly mentioned as the two greatest commandments (e.g., Matthew 22:37-39). For this reason marriage (Ephesians 5:25; Colossians 3:19), the family, the church, and relationships all the way up to enemies are to be marked by love: "Love must be sincere . . . Honor one another above yourselves . . . Bless those who persecute you; bless and do not curse . . . On the contrary: If your enemy is hungry, feed him; if he is thirsty, give him something to drink . . ." (Romans 12: 9-20a). For this reason Jesus says in the Sermon on the Mount: "Love your enemies, do good to those who hate you" (Luke 6:27; similarly 6:35; Matthew 5:44).

The idea in the Bible that love particularly expresses itself in sacrifice is unknown in the Koran. In the Bible we meet the idea of sacrifice, especially with the death of Jesus. It is God himself who seals the greatest love of all time by the greatest sacrifice of all time (1 John 4:9-10; John 3:16), but it also applies to people, for instance when Jesus says: "Greater love has no one than this, that he lay down his life for his friend" (John 15:13). For this reason the secret of marriage is, in the final instance, the readiness to sacrifice one's life for the other out of love (Ephesians 5:25, 28).

There is also a deeper difference between the understanding of love in Christianity and all other religions, and it has to do with the Trinity and thereby with the relationships among the Father, Son and Holy Spirit. In the Trinity love itself first becomes possible "within God" as an uncreated reality. It is not a reality that first has to create a counterpart in order to be able to love. More will be said on this below.

The emphasis on the love of God is also the reason why God in the New Testament is repeatedly described as "Father" and why Christians name him "our Father" or "dear Father" ("Abba, Father" in Romans 8:15b) in prayer as well as why the parable of the prodigal son emphatically describes that God is a father who invites his lost children back home (Luke 15:11-32).

God: Lord or Friend and Brother?

*According to the **Koran** there is a great distance between mankind and God. For that reason a person can never become God's friend or brother.*

In the **Bible** God is allowed to be called friend and Father by mankind, and Jesus is designated as friend and brother.

In the **Koran** God can graciously come to mankind, and mankind answers with thankfulness and with acknowledgement, but this obedience towards God can never diminish the cleft between Creator and creature. A person could never become a child, a brother, or a friend of God.

Sura 6:127 possibly names God a "friend" of believers while others translate it as "protector." What is meant is that he prepares a living place for believers in Paradise. In Sura 7:155 Moses calls God his "friend" (here also others translate this with "protector") and asks him for mercy. Muslim theology emphasizes that this is an exception for Moses that does not apply to anyone else.

People are allowed to call God "Father" and "friend" in the **Bible**. Titus 3:4 speaks of the: "kindness and love of God our Savior," and 1 Peter 2:3 calls God "good." Jesus the Son of God "is not ashamed" to call believers "friends" (John 15:14-15; Luke 12:4) and "brothers" (Hebrews 2:11). Indeed everyone who receives Jesus receives the right to be called "children of God" (John 1:12), because they are "dearly loved children" (Ephesians 5:1). Moses speaks with God "as a man speaks with his friend" (Deuteronomy 33:11). God is Abraham's "friend" (James 2:23), and elsewhere he is God's "beloved" (Isaiah 41:8). Paul writes the Letter to the Romans to "all . . . who are loved by God" (Romans 1:7; similarly Colossians 3:12; 2 Thessalonians 2:13). And Jesus often calls people his friends (e.g., Luke 12:4).

The Founder of the Religion: Warlord or Peacemaker?

*In the **Koran** the founder of the religion is very much a politician and a warlord. The goal is to unite faith and politics and to place the state under the organized people of God.*

In the **Bible** the founder of the religion declines political activity and dies for the salvation of the world. The tasks of the church and state are different, and Christians are to place themselves under the non-Christian constitutional state, even if they should bring know-how into politics and society.

The **Koran** reports how Mohammed went from being a derided prophet to head of state in the last ten years of his life (622-632 A.D.) in Medina. He did this through what he was proclaiming as well as through wars. It also reports how he became lord over a growing empire. Islamic governance demonstrated a unified spiritual and worldly regency when Mohammed was still alive. This is not the place to go into the life story of Mohammed and his successors in more detail, and Islam has indeed accounted for various state forms over the course of its history. However, from the way its scriptures are composed, Islam always seeks that not only the Mosque but the state as well be both placed under Islamic law and that the entire creation and social reality be molded by the Koran.

The portion of the **Bible** containing the New Testament reports that the proclamation and work of Jesus was marked by non-violence, whereby he decidedly distanced himself from many groups that propagated the idea of a political overthrow by the use of violence. While the Jewish expectations were hopeful of a Messiah to bring Israel into political domination over all the world, Jesus' instruments for the expansion of the Kingdom of God were the repentance and conversion of each individual, not revolution and coercion, "for all who draw the sword will die by the sword" (Matthew 26:52b). Jesus clearly said: "Blessed are the peacemakers, for they will be called children of God" (Matthew 5:9) and "My kingdom is not of this world" (John 18:36a). Jesus backed the separation of the offices of king and priest in the Old Testament that prepared the way for a separation of church and state when he said: "Give to Caesar what is Caesar's and to God what is God's" (Matthew 22:21b; Mark 12:17; Luke 20). Paul subordinates the church to the Roman State (Romans 13:1-7). What is referred to as "God's servant" is not the Christian church in this context. Rather, it is the state that also punishes Christians who do evil.

In its two thousand year history and global geographic expansion, Christianity has probably gone through each and every thinkable variety of relationship between religion and the state and has made many mistakes along the way. However, looking at it from the basic structure, the Christian church can only see one spiritual task, which it can best exercise the less political and economic power it holds in its hands. As a prophetic alerter and ethical advocate, the church can provide the state a good service, and God-fearing people, such as Joseph and Daniel, can assume an important role that is beneficial to society. However, the church itself does not have a claim on political power.

The Founder of the Religion: Master or Servant?

*In the **Koran** the founder of the religion, who is also a prophet, rises to be a successful lord and warlord. He triumphs, and through his success his actions are authenticated. God is Lord, and that means that he does not serve.*

In the **Bible** the founder of the religion rises up to become a servant of mankind. In the Bible the founder suffers and God authenticates his sacrifice through the resurrection. God is Lord, and for that reason he is able to serve mankind.

Regarding the **Koran,** please see the prior section.

In the **Bible** a high value is placed on service. Peace for Christians does not arise through oppression and the exercise of power, but rather through relinquishment (1 Corinthians 6:7), by valuing others more highly (Philippians 2:3), and by service (Galatians 5:13). Jesus says of himself: "For even the Son of Man did not come to be served, but to serve, and to give his life as a ransom for many" (Matthew 20:28; Mark 10:45). He draws the following conclusion for the coming leaders of the church: ". . . whoever wants to become great among you must be your servant" (Matthew 20:26; Mark 10:43; similarly Matthew 23:11; Mark 9:35; Luke 22:26). "For whoever exalts himself will be humbled, and whoever humbles himself will be exalted" (Matthew 23:12). Jesus, the "servant" (Luke 22:27, 1 Corinthians 12:5) taught Peter to serve, such that Peter later writes that people are to "serve others" (1 Peter 4:10).

Is Prayer above All a Communal Duty or a Personal Conversation with the Father?

*Prayer in the **Koran** is the most important expression of the relationship one has to God, i.e., submission to God. There are daily required prayers that are central, pre-formulated, and precisely prescribed in a ritualistic manner. This is the case even though self-formulated prayers are also possible.*

Prayer in the **Bible** is the most important expression of the relationship one has to God. Self-formulated prayers made directly to God are central, even if there are liturgical prayers of all kinds that are desirable and are even contained in the Bible in large numbers. "Private" prayer stands before any prayer in community.

The **Koran** and Islamic tradition (Hadith) prescribe required prayers for believers at five specific times throughout the day, and woes are proclaimed on those who do not comply (Sura 107:4-5). Ibn Rassoul writes: "Beginning with the seventh year of life, children should be exhorted by their parents to hold to saying prayers, and from the tenth year of life held to saying prayers with blows to the body if it is not possible by other means."[46] This does not exclude individual prayers in Islam: "One differentiates between the actual required prayers (fard), which on no account may be omitted, and the so-called sunna prayers, which precede or follow. Nafl prayers are completely voluntary prayers."[47] "After prayer, one may remain seated in meditation, and it is Sunna that one may formulate in one's own words and offer as prayers of supplication."[48] Still, the following applies to such individual prayers: "Prayer in community is more valuable that individual prayer."[49]

Prayer in the **Bible** is always voluntary. There are no required prayers, and there are no fixed instructions regarding times, rituals, or contents, as much as a well ordered prayer life is helpful. The Holy Spirit brings about the desire in an individual to turn to God with all concerns and represents the individual before God (Romans 8:26). It is a personal conversation with God and a great privilege, since the unsaved sinner is not worthy to come before God. It is only due to the fact that Jesus represents the praying individual before God and cleanses him from "all unrighteousness" (1 John 1:9), and because the Holy Spirit "helps us in our weakness" and translates our "groans" (Romans 8:26a), that the believer can come before the "throne of grace" (Hebrews 4:16).

Everyone who wants to pray can turn to God at anytime and anywhere with requests. The praying individual often expects direction, wisdom, and answers from God, while prayer in Islam does not expect or ask for an answer from Allah. Since according to the biblical notion God is the Father of his children, he does them good (Matthew 7:9) and hears their petitions. God's children are able to approach God with the intimate address "dear Father" ("Abba Father" in Romans 8:15). A special promise is made by God regarding prayer that is offered in consent and in a community of believers (Matthew 18:19-20).

---

[46] Rassoul, As-Salah: *Das Gebet*, p. 21.
[47] islam.de/27.php.
[48] Rassoul, As-Salah: *Das Gebet*, p. 99.
[49] Op. cit., p. 105 documented from tradition.

Even as Jesus was giving his disciples the most important liturgical prayer in the Sermon on the Mount, the Lord's Prayer (Matthew 6:9-13), he said: "And when you pray, do not keep on babbling like pagans, for they think they will be heard because of their many words" (Matthew 6:7). Jesus also called upon his hearers not to pray in order to be seen (Matthew 6:5). Rather, he taught: "But when you pray, go into your room, close the door and pray to your Father, who is unseen" (Matthew 6:6).

Koran or Jesus? A Book or a Person?

*Next to God in the center of **Islam** is the Koran, that is to say, a book, because it was sent from eternity into the world.*

Next to God in the center of **Christianity** is Jesus Christ, that is to say, a person, because this individual was sent from eternity into the world.

Even though the **Bible** and the **Koran** were compared above as "God's word" in the way they view themselves, in a certain sense the Bible actually is not the correct counterpart to the Koran. "In an inter-religious comparison, the Koran cannot really be placed next to the Bible. Rather, the Koran can only be placed next to Jesus, even though there are many differences that become visible. 'What Jesus is for Christianity, the Koran is for orthodox Islam.'"[50] Stated another way: "In the center of Christianity there is a person, Jesus Christ. In contrast one finds in the center of Islam a book, the Koran."[51] This has to do with the fact that in Islam the Koran comes directly from God's eternity. In Christianity it is not the historically developed Bible that comes from eternity. Rather, it is Jesus, the Son of God, who comes from eternity.

There is, however, a limitation to the comparison. Hans Zirker states it as follows: "When only a comparison is made, not enough attention is given to how Christianity confesses that there was an 'incarnation' of the word of God, that God became man, while in Islam there is an 'inlibration,' or a book's becoming. This analogy is indeed justified, insofar as in Jesus Christ Christianity sees an unsurpassable revelation. Islam sees the same in the Koran. At the same time there is a serious difference, which puts the term 'inlibration' into question: 'the mother of the book,' the heavenly book, remains with God and is itself not sent to mankind, rather, it is the Koran . . .; now more than ever God remains as before the absolutely transcendent Creator separated from all creation. For this reason the message that is God's word in the Koran does not bring God himself into a

---

[50] Zirker, *Koran*, p. 45.
[51] Louis Gardet, *Der Islam*, Köln: J. P. Bachem, 1968, p. 39.

historically worldly presence where he can be experienced. Revelation for Islam is not the self-revelation of God."[52]

Is the Founder Above or Beneath the Holy Scriptures?

*In **Islam** the founder Mohammed is under the Holy Scriptures. He receives his meaning from the Scriptures since he receives them and proclaims them.*

In **Christianity** the founder is above the Holy Scriptures. They receive their meaning from him. Jesus is the actual "word of God," and the Scriptures, as the "word of God," testify of him.

In the Koran Mohammed is himself confirmed by the miracle of the Koran. His significance is that he is completely subordinate to God's word and is only the messenger and prophet. When Mohammed was neither acknowledged by his Arabian compatriots nor by the Jews and Christians as a prophet of God, and when the threatened judgment did not occur, he had to endure increasing ridicule and threats in his hometown of Mecca. Mohammed's contemporaries demanded that he produce a miracle as had all earlier prophets (Sura 20:133). Instead, Mohammed referred to the Koran as his miracle, which his contemporaries initially did not acknowledge (Sura 11, 13;10, 37-38). This is the reason Mohammed demanded that they produce a document comparable to the Koran, which they in turn could not do (Sura 17:88). Islamic theology calls this "the certifying miracle." It is the miracle that proves Mohammed's prophetic office.

In the **Bible** Jesus, as God's Son, is never set against written revelation. On the other hand, it is made clear that Jesus' incarnation fulfills all written revelation as well as the entire story of salvation and at the same time surpasses everything. In Hebrews 1:1-4 one reads: "In the past God spoke to our forefathers through the prophets at many times and in various ways, but in these last days he has spoken to us by his Son, whom he appointed heir of all things, and through whom he made the universe."

The Apostle Paul himself writes: "For we know in part and we prophesy in part, but when perfection comes, the imperfect disappears" (1 Corinthians 13: 9-10). Islamic revelation could never be viewed as "in part!" What does this "perfection" mean for Paul? It is the remaining encounter with Jesus Christ himself: "Now we see but a poor reflection as in a mirror;

---

[52] Zirker, *Koran*, pp. 49-50.

II. A Relationship With God and How it Emerges Through His Word

then we shall see face to face. Now I know in part; then I shall know fully, even as I am fully known" (1 Corinthians 13:12).

The Catholic World Catechism writes in this connection: "Still, the Christian faith is not a 'religion of the book.' Christianity is the religion of the 'Word' of God, a word which is 'not a written and mute word, but the Word which is incarnate and living.' If the Scriptures are not to remain a dead letter, Christ, the eternal Word of the living God, must, through the Holy Spirit, 'open [our] minds (Luke 24:45) to understand the Scriptures'" (§108).

According to New Testament testimony, Jesus is the "word of God" (John 1:1-3; Hebrews 11:1). In Jesus, God speaks in his most originally underlying form. For this reason theology has unanimously seen Christ as "Lord of the Scriptures." For instance, Jesus is "Lord of the Sabbath" (Matthew 12:8), although one can read about the Sabbath "in the law" (Matthew 12:5).

That Jesus is the Word of God is often used today as a reason for saying that the Holy Scriptures cannot be God's word. But the same Scriptures that Jesus calls the word of God say first of all that Jesus speaks "God's word" (John 3:34; 17:8; comp. 8:28-29, 31-32, 46-47). Secondly, Jesus himself calls the "Scriptures" "God's word" (e.g., Mark 7:10-13) and the like and makes far-reaching statements about the "Scriptures" in a manner that authorizes them as God's speaking (e.g., John 10:34; Mark 12:10; Mark 12:24). That Jesus is the Word of God does not abolish the divine inspiration of the Holy Scriptures. However, it does make it clear that the actual revelation of God took place through the incarnation of God in his Son and that the Holy Scriptures are only to be understood always and exclusively within the framework of the personal relationship to God and to his Son.

Christendom worships its founder in the same way that it worships God himself. For the church, Jesus is not only the originator and rediscoverer of metaphysical and ethical teachings, such as Buddha or Confucius, and not only an envoy of God to whom God revealed himself, such as Moses or Mohammed, nor is he the incarnation of the lord of the world, such as Krishna. Rather, he is all of these things taken together and in addition God himself. By his birth, crucifixion, resurrection and ascension, Jesus is the center and turning point of world history. Furthermore, as the judge of the world at the time of the Last Judgment and center of eternal community with God, he is the goal of world history. Jesus neither only stands at the beginning of the Christian message nor is he only its facilitator. Rather, he is the one who produced the foundation for Christianity and is the message itself.

A Celebration for the Holy Scriptures?

The fact that the Koran and Jesus should be compared to each other becomes clear with the annual commemorations that are conducted in Islam and in Christianity.

*The sending down of the **Koran** is celebrated as an important Islamic holiday.*

*Christianity does not have a holiday for the **Bible** but rather only for Jesus Christ.*

In **Islam**, next to the Festival of Sacrifice that constitutes the end of the pilgrimage to Mecca, the supreme Islamic holiday is the celebration of fast-breaking at the end of the month of fasting called Ramadan. Ramadan is celebrated due to the fact that it is in this month that Mohammed received the first revelations of the Koran (Sura 2:185). Towards the end of Ramadan (mostly in the night of the twenty-sixth to the twenty-seventh of the month), the "Night of Decree" (Arabic *tanzîl*) or the "Night of Power" (Arabic *laylatu l-qadr*) is celebrated (Sure 97:1-4; 44:2).

Christianity does not have a holiday or any other sort of central ceremony for the Bible. All important holidays such as Christmas, Good Friday, and Easter have to do with Jesus Christ and his earthly ministry as the Son of God. Pentecost, which is the celebration of Jesus' sending the Holy Spirit in his place, is the exception.

Jesus: Prophet or God and Provider of Salvation?

*Since the **Koran** came about later than the Bible, and for that reason repeatedly addresses and judges the Bible, the difference between the religions' founders understandings of themselves also becomes clear by the fact that the Jesus of the Koran is presented as a prophet subordinate to Mohammed and the Koran. The exceptional position that Jesus assumes in Christianity is sharply repudiated.*

According to the Christian understanding, in the **Bible** Jesus is God himself. He became a man and as God's Son he suffered substitutionally for mankind, died, rose again, and thereby brought salvation. In Jesus Christ the word of God became flesh.

In the **Koran** it is unthinkable that a creature could take on divine attributes or receive a part of the divine nature of the Creator. It is just as un-

II. A Relationship With God and How it Emerges Through His Word 61

thinkable that God could step out of his position of transcendence and take on human characteristics. For this reason, it is unfathomable in the Koran that God in Jesus Christ could become a creature and an individual. In doing so, God would become equal to man and as a man would be subject to the conditions of earthly life. The facts that Jesus ate, drank, slept and felt pain, desperation, and sadness like any other person operate for Muslim theologians as evidences against the divinity of Jesus.

Jesus Christ (Arabic Isa Masih) is one of the most important prophets in the Koran, even if he is placed under Mohammed. Jesus announces Mohammed as his direct successor (Sura 61:6), a mortal man, who was sent to the Israelites with a scripture (Sura 5:46), the Indjil (gospel). He was born of Mary, who was a God-fearing virgin, and he proclaimed faith in the one true God, announced the coming judgment, gave alms and said the ritualistic Islamic prayer. By God's speaking he is the created "word of God," "his word" (Sura 4:171), "servant of God" (Sura 4:172), "prophet" (Sura 19:30) and "apostle" (Sura 4:157). He performed miracles, raised the dead, healed the sick, gave life to dead matter, and he will return to the earth at the end of time.

The Koran mentions as little regarding the central contents of Jesus' teachings, which are reported in the New Testament (the Sermon on the Mount, for instance), as it does about his relationship with his disciples. The disciples are referred to in the Koran in short as "helpers of God" (Sura 3:52). Jesus' mission is not mentioned in connection with the question of salvation. He is not crucified. Rather, he is raptured alive to heaven. Jesus is also not the Son of God, nor is he a member of the Trinity, nor can he forgive sins.

The central message in the New Testament portion of the **Bible** is that God himself became man in the person of Jesus Christ (1 John 4:2; 2 John 1:7) and that the eternal "word" became "flesh" (John 1:14). In the vein of traditional Christian theology, Christology, as it binds the Christian confessions can be formulated as follows: "The Son of God, who is the second person of the Trinity, and who is true and eternal God, is of one essence with the Father and is equal to him, did take upon himself in the fullness of time a human nature with all its essential characteristics and general weaknesses, albeit without sin. By the power of the Holy Spirit he was conceived in the body of and out of the essence of the virgin Mary, such that two perfect and different natures, divine and human, were inseparably united in one person without change, mixture or commingling. This person is true God and true man, yet a single Christ, who is the sole mediator between God and man.[53]

This is the reason that one cannot worship God and at the same time reject Jesus. Rather, to worship God means to follow Jesus and to worship him as God. In John 8:37-59 contemporaries declare their uncompromising monotheism to Jesus: "The only Father we have is God himself" (John 8:41b). And Jesus answers them at once: "If God were your Father, you would love me, for I came from God and now am here. I have not come on my own; but he sent me" (John 8:42; compare 8:55-58). Jesus' hearers were annoyed, because Jesus "was even calling God his own Father, making himself equal with God" (John 5:18; compare 17-47). Jesus also understood the Old Testament in this manner and for this reason said to his detractors God's word does not "dwell in you, for you do not believe the one he sent. You diligently study the Scriptures because you think that by them you possess eternal life. These are the Scriptures that testify about me" (John 5:38-39). Therefore, in the final event Moses (and respectively, the Torah) will also be a witness against the rejection of Christ (John 5:45-46).

Jesus Christ	
The Koran as well as the Bible speak of Jesus, whom God sent to Israel. The Koran and the Bible call him "Christ." He was born of the virgin Mary and performed miracles in Israel. He ascended into heaven and will return to earth at the end of time to judge all people. He receives the highest titles among all those who have been sent by God.	
Koran	**Bible**
1. The title "**Christ**" (Messiah) is used 11 times as a supplement to the name of Jesus. However, it is used only as a name and not with its (biblical) meaning of Savior and Anointed One (Sura 3:45).	1. The title "Christ" (Messiah) means: the one anointed with the Holy Spirit, the "anointed one;" he unites the Old Testament offices of priest, prophet and king in the Son of God, who is sent into the world to save it (Luke 1:26-38; 3:21-22).
2. Jesus (Arabic *Isa*) was created by God by his word ("Be!") and by God's power placed in the virgin Mary. He is only a human (Sura 3:59; 5:75; 5:116-117).	2. Jesus was begotten by the Holy Spirit in the virgin Mary and is simultaneously truly man and truly God (Luke 1:35). As God he is He uncreated and exists from eternity to eter-

---

[53] Schirrmacher, *Evangelische Glaube*, Art. 8.2.

	nity (Micah 5:1; Hebrews 7:3).
3. Jesus was only a prophet, even if he was one of the most important prophets in history. Mohammed is, however, more important than Jesus. Mohammed is the "seal of the prophets" (33:40; 61:6). Mohammed's coming is already announced in the Old Testament by Moses and Isaiah and in the New Testament by Jesus (Sura 2:67ff; 7,157).	3. **Jesus** came into the world as the Savior promised in the Old Testament. As the son of God he is the greatest prophet and the center of all prophecy, and he proclaims the coming of the Holy Spirit (John 14:16). Mohammed is not mentioned in the Bible and does not comply with the biblical criteria for a prophet (Acts 10:43).
4. **Jesus** was not crucified and was not resurrected. A crucifixion would have been a disgraceful defeat for him. He could not have brought salvation by his death. Most Muslims believe that Jesus now lives in heaven (Sura 4:157-158).	4. **Jesus** died on the cross. He was placed in a tomb and was raised from the dead on the third day. He ascended into heaven, where he lives today and rules. By his death he achieved victory over the powers of sin and death (1 Peter 1:18-19; Ephesians 2:18).

The Trinity: Polytheism or the Nature of God?

*The **Koran** maintains that the Christian teaching that Jesus is not only a prophet and teacher but God himself, as well as the closely related teaching about the Trinity, is polytheism.*

The church has summarized the **Bible**'s teaching as follows: "In the unity of the Godhead there are three persons with one essence, one power and one eternity – God the Father, God the Son, and God the Holy Spirit. The Father is born of no one nor is the Father derived from anyone; the Son is born eternally from the Father; the Holy Spirit proceeds eternally from[54] the Father and the Son."[55]

The **Koran** and Islam deny that Christianity is actually a monotheistic religion. This is due to the following: "The most important concept in Islam, and the source of all its other principles and approaches, is the unity

---

[54] The suffix "from the Son" (*filioque*) was added later and is historically justifiably rejected by orthodox churches.
[55] Schirrmacher, *Evangelische Glaube*, Art. 2.3.

of God (Tauhid). Monotheism is most purely depicted in Islam."[56] Even when the Koran frequently differentiates between actual idolaters, who are to be outright rejected and fought, and the adherents of the better religions (such as Christians and Jews) that are in written form, these better religions are given a status subordinate to Islam. Still, idolaters and Christians are often mentioned together (e.g., Sura 98:1, 6).

The Trinity is sharply rejected: "Certainly they disbelieve who say: Surely Allah is the third (person) of the three; and there is no god but the one God, and if they desist not from what they say, a painful chastisement shall befall those among them who disbelieve... The Messiah, son of Marium is but an apostle" (Sura 5:73, 75). "O followers of the Book! do not exceed the limits in your religion, and do not speak (lies) against Allah, but (speak) the truth; the Messiah, Isa son of Marium is only an apostle of Allah and His Word which He communicated to Marium and a spirit from Him; ... say not, Three. Desist, it is better for you; Allah is only one God; far be it from His glory that He should have a son..." (Sura 4:171-172).

The teaching that is drawn from the **Bible** that God is triune and was formulated at the Council of Nicea (325 A.D.), with the teaching that Jesus is truly man and truly God as it was formulated at the Council of Chalcedon (451 A.D.), count as the decisive teachings that have always united the various Christian confessions. It was something that was never disputed during the Reformation. However, the Trinity has never been understood as something that was devised by councils. Rather, the Trinity has been viewed as something that was taught in particular in the New Testament. The confessions were viewed as declaring what was taught in the New Testament to be true and to be presenting it in complementary fashion and in a summarized form. For instance, such teachings in the New Testament are found when in the instructions to baptize the obligation is noted to do so in the single "name" (singular), which is "the name of the Father and of the Son and of the Holy Spirit" (Matthew 28:19). In Galatians 4:6 one reads: "Because you are sons, God (the Father) sent the Spirit (Holy Spirit) of his Son (Jesus) into our hearts, the Spirit who calls out, "Abba, Father."

As regards the rapprochement of content of the great monotheistic religions, this is only possible where the teaching of the Trinity and the associated teaching of the divinity of Jesus are removed from the top of the agenda in Christian theology and mission. The German word *Dreieinigkeit* shows very clearly that the biblical teaching of the Trinity stands over against two other views of God. In the German word the *ein* (from *eins*, or

---

[56] www.way-to-allah.com/islam_zum_kennenlernen/was_ist_islam.html.

one) stands over against polytheism, and the *drei* (three) likewise stands over against 'monistic monotheism' (an only-one-God-belief).

The Bible states that "God is love" (1 John 4:8, 16). The teaching of the Trinity has a different meaning in Christianity than it does in other religions. The love between Father, Son and Spirit is, namely, the starting point of all thought regarding love (John 17:24). Love always includes at least two agents. Love means precisely to speak, to decide, and to act for the benefit of another. There can only be practiced love in monistic monotheism when God has produced a counterpart. In Trinitarian monotheism the persons within the Trinity have loved themselves since eternity, long before a counterpart was created. The persons of the Trinity love each other, speak with each other, and act for each other.

Since mankind is made in the image of God, the eternal community of love in God in the Bible is the standard and starting point for community among mankind. People speak with each other, because God is one who speaks with others. People should work for each other, because God himself is one who works and lives for others.

Excursus: How God comes near according to the Bible

In the Christian faith God comes near mankind with his revelation. He comes to mankind. He speaks to mankind. He speaks with mankind. He speaks the language of men, and he gives a stable basis to the relationship between God and mankind in which he binds himself to his work, as the one who is absolute and true, who enables faith and trust. It is for this very reason that God's progressive revelation found in the salvation narrative also has a written version, which makes the reliability of God palpable and brings God near to all mankind in human language.

For its part, written revelation pushes for fulfillment in a manner in which God comes *even closer* to us: God became man and "made his dwelling among us" (John 1:14). In Christ God becomes "Immanuel," "God with us" (Matthew 1:23). For this reason God's incarnation in Jesus does not suspend the written revelation. Rather, it fulfils it with the actual word of God.

And still this is not enough! God wants to come even nearer to us. Jesus, who is true man and true God, leaves the earth with his new body after his resurrection. In his place he sends the *Holy Spirit*, which can not only come nearer to all humanity than Jesus; rather, since Pentecost, he lives in believers, so that God's spirit witnesses to their spirit and gives them inner power to live according to God's will (Romans 8:3-4). God cannot come any nearer to us!

The three steps of God
1. God comes close to men, speaking man's language, revealing himself to them, and giving his will to them in written form.
2. God comes even closer to men by taking on bodily form in Christ and revealing himself directly to man.
3. God comes even closer to men by living through his Spirit in those who believe in Jesus Christ.

For a Muslim it is really difficult to understand that the Bible is simultaneously man's word and God's word, since a Muslim can only think of God's word as something without human assistance. It is even more difficult for a Muslim to comprehend that in Jesus Christ God and man are conjoined, all the more so because the Muslim is marked by the idea that that can only mean idolatry.

As much as this point stands in the center of the denial of Christianity, since the Koran sees the primary evil of Christians in the fact that they assign to the human prophet Jesus the status of God's Son, experience shows that the next step even more definitively exceeds the imagination of a Muslim. That is, namely, that Christians believe that God's spirit is the third person of the one true God and lives in the believer.

Is Sin Committed only Against People or Above All Against God?

*In the **Koran** sin is wrong action against oneself and not against God.*

In the **Bible** sin is in the final instance always directed toward God, even when it hurts one's neighbor.

In the **Koran** Adam and his wife sin in Paradise, but they confess their sin such that God again showed them the straight path (Sura 2:37), since they sinned in a manner that they said of themselves, "We have been unjust to ourselves" (Sura 7:23). Of the sin of ungratefulness of the children of Israel the following is written: "And we made the clouds to give shade over you and we sent to you manna and quails: Eat of the good things that We have given you; and they did not do us (God) any harm, but they made their own souls suffer the loss" (Sura 2:57). Correspondingly, death is not a consequence of sin (Sura 2:35-39).

Sin in the **Bible** in the final instance always directed toward God himself. In the famous Psalm of repentance (Psalm 51), King David acknowledges murder and adultery: "Against you, you only, have I sinned and done what is evil in your sight (Psalm 51:4a; comp. 1 Kings 8:50). The Old Testament frequently compares the relationship between God and Israel with marriage and Israel's falling away from God as adultery. God is angered about the sin of mankind and at the same time grieved: "Yet they rebelled and grieved his Holy Spirit" (Isaiah 63:10; comp. Ephesians 4:30). In his holy anger Jesus was also always distressed (Mark 3:5 and John 11:33).

Is Sin an Isolated Act or is Original Sin the Foundational Rupture in the Relationship with God?

*In every case, sin in the **Koran** is an individual act and is overcome by leaving it behind from that point onwards. There is no original sin, and there is no notion that only God could help in overcoming sin.*

The **Bible** views sin above all not as an isolated act but rather in its aggregate as the breaking of a covenant between God and mankind. It is also a mark of mankind's infidelity toward God. Mankind is unable to free himself without the aid of God.

In the **Koran** Adam's "fall" (Sura 2:36) has no consequences for all mankind. Islam and the Koran do not have the notion of an actual "fall of mankind" just as little as there is "original sin," since "no bearer of burden shall bear the burden of another" (Sura 39:7). For this reason there exists no necessity for deliverance from original sin. When man forgets God's commands, strays from them, or obeys the "whispers" of Satan, who is an egregious "enemy" of mankind (Sura 35:6), he indeed commits a sinful act. However, he is not basically lost as a result, nor is he fallen or separated from God. When he again remembers God's commandments and takes refuge in God, he is in the position to again do good. Full of grace and with mercy, God again turns to the individual.

Abdoldjavad Falaturi writes: "According to the Koran, mankind by his created nature is geared towards God. He is not burdened with sinfulness. Adam's sin was forgiven by his contrition. This model is valid for everyone. In Islam the act of deliverance is replaced by divine mercy."[57]

Evil is not found within people or in their nature. Rather, it is only a temptation that comes to people from the outside. "The view of man as found in the Koran is at first glance one that above all appears to be

---

[57] Abdoldjavad Falaturi in *WDR*, *Koran*, p. 46.

marked by character weakness. Yet in principle it is through and through optimistic and positive. This is due to the notion that in the final instance weaknesses are interpreted as unbelief."[58] Detail has been provided as to the consequences this has for the question of superiority and self-criticism, respectively.

The **Bible** views sin first of all not as an individual transgression. Rather, the Bible views sin in its entirety as a breaking of a covenant between God and man and as man's infidelity toward God (in particular in Romans 1:17-32). Sin is not so much understood from the aspect of individual, wicked deeds, but rather from the aspect of original sin. It is for this reason that deliverance from sin is not so much understood as deliverance from a particular sin but as deliverance from the sinfulness of man and from enmity towards God.

Original sin[59] is a teaching that is only known in Christianity. It says not only that an individual sins. Rather, it says that mankind is already marked by sin prior to the individual's committing the first sin. This inherited state of being outside of God's grace was unleashed by the fall of the first humans, Adam and Eve (Genesis 3). This is also what necessitates collective salvation by the new Adam, Jesus Christ. Via his concrete, personal transgression, each person confirms that there is original sin but he or she does not cause it.

Evil can be found in people themselves. "For from within, out of men's hearts, come evil thoughts, sexual immorality, theft, murder, adultery, greed, malice, deceit, lewdness, envy, slander, arrogance and folly. All these evils come from inside and make a man 'unclean'" (Mark 7:21-23). Mankind is basically not in the position to not sin, since he is "sold" (Romans 7:14-15) to sin. Paul declares, "For what I do is not the good I want to do; no, the evil I do not want to do—this I keep on doing" (Romans 7:19).

Mankind remains under the curse of sin and will always repeatedly do evil until he accepts that he cannot really improve himself. He must see that Jesus' death on the cross also occurred as atonement for his sins. Only then does the Holy Spirit take up residence in him, and the sinner can then withstand sin. If he nevertheless sins– and this occurs again and again in

---

[58] Tilman Nagel, *Der Koran, Einführung – Texte – Erläuterungen*, München: C.H.Beck, 1998³, p. 253.

[59] With few exceptions Christian confessions are basically consistent with the teaching of original sin. However, they considerably depart from each other in the question of the extent to which original sin affected mankind.

the life of a Christian – and asks for forgiveness of his sins, he experiences forgiveness and new fellowship with his Creator (1 John 1:9).

Does Conversion Occur by Confession or by Receipt of Salvation?

In Islam as well as in Christianity, there are different understandings of how one comes to faith in the respective faiths. These different understandings follow from differing understandings of sin.

*According to the **Koran** and in Islam, how does one become a Muslim? By submitting to God's will. Above all, this occurs by reciting the confession of faith in Arabic.*

*According to the **Bible**, one becomes a Christian by calling upon the name of the Lord Jesus Christ, by deeply trusting God while asking God for forgiveness of one's sins, and by entering into a covenant with God and with the community of the children of God.*

The view of the **Koran** was already presented above in the sections on "faith" and the confession of faith.

The view of the **Bible** was likewise discussed under "faith." Externally this occurs by baptism and by the first participation in the Lord's Supper. Saying the confession of faith can play a role. What is decisive, however, is that both sacraments stand for the fact that Jesus suffered for us, died, was raised, and that we are brought into covenant with him and his church if we place our faith in him.

The Central Theme of the Holy Scriptures: is it Submission or Salvation?

In Islam as well as in Christianity there are different understandings of the central theme of revelation that follow from differing understandings of sin.

*The central theme of the **Koran** and the reason why it was at all revealed is submission to God, which is the sole manner of being preserved in the judgment. This is what gives the religion its name: "Islam."*

*The central theme of the **Bible** and the reason why it was inspired and why it testifies to God's revelation in Jesus Christ is reconciliation with God in Christ, which alone can preserve a person in the judgment. This is what gives the religion its name: "Christianity."*

Above all, the **Koran** serves as a warning of judgment to unbelievers and the call that they should submit to God and his will. This is expressed in particular in Suras 34-114 from the early time in Mecca. This is the task of every prophet in history, including Moses and Jesus. Mankind has to simply leave his mistaken ways and acknowledge that there is only one God and that Mohammed is his prophet. Mankind also has to live according to God's will. With this he is preserved in the judgment.

In the **Bible** the central theme of the entire "Scriptures" is the salvation of mankind. Paul calls upon Timothy to continue in the "holy Scriptures," which he knew from infancy. Writing to Timothy Paul says that the Scriptures are "able to make you wise for salvation through faith in Christ Jesus" (2 Timothy 3:14-15). It is not by accident that these words come directly prior to the statement (according to the Latin translation) to which we owe our concept of "inspiration": "All Scripture is God-breathed and is useful . . ." (2 Timothy 3:16). For Paul, the meaning of the Bible is therefore only understandable in connection with salvation in Christ. It is not the word of God that saves us. Rather, it is Jesus Christ alone and our trust in him. However, the Bible does make us wise unto salvation, which is in Jesus Christ. It does not do more than that, but it also does not do less. What would we know about Jesus Christ and his work of redemption if God had not given this to us in written form? What would be the value of a written version if Jesus had not actually become a man and had not truly redeemed us?

Does Forgiveness come by Obedience or by the Reconciling Action of God?

*In the **Koran** if the penitent sinner changes course and leaves his sin, he is forgiven due to mercy. In order to receive forgiveness, neither a special teaching nor a special ritual is required.*

In the **Bible** no one can receive forgiveness without God's taking action. However, since God in Jesus Christ carried mankind's sin to the cross, a person can receive forgiveness and new life. Large portions of theology have to do with forgiveness, and the largest part of Christian ritual revolves around this issue.

Since "Allah is Forgiving, Merciful" (Sura 57:28), in the **Koran** a person receives God's forgiveness after he has committed a sin, turns again to God, is remorseful of his sin, and makes the resolution to avoid this sin in the future (Sura 3:135-136). The Koran warns about punishment for those who do not turn to Allah. Neither in the Koran nor in the tradition that has been passed down is there, however, any prayer in which the sinner thanks God for forgiveness that is received. The fact of the matter is that the believer indeed expects God's forgiveness, but to adjudicate it to oneself or to accept it as a fact would be tantamount to limiting the absolute sovereignty of God.

In the Old Testament of the **Bible**, forgiveness and reconciliation are achieved by sacrifices which are in the center of the faith and its ceremonies. In the Bible's New Testament forgiveness is possible only by Jesus Christ's sacrifice on the cross, whereby the sinner is made righteous before God (Romans 1:17). The most important sacraments, baptism and the Lord's Supper, revolve around forgiveness of sins in Jesus Christ.

From the beginning, Christians understood Jesus' death as a substitutionary sacrifice for the sins of mankind. Out of love for sinners, the sinless and innocent Jesus was delivered unto death by God himself in order to pay for sin's guilt. The death of Christ is the price for redemption (Romans 3:24; Galatians 3:13; Ephesians 1:7; 1 Peter 1:18-19). With repeatedly new pictures – from the slave market, from the courts, from the military, from services in the temple, and from daily relationships – the New Testament describes believers' reconciliation with God through the death of Jesus Christ. Redemption is expressed as deliverance from sin and a changed life reflecting newfound freedom.

Submission or Reconciliation?

*In the **Koran** the best relationship to God is that of submission on the part of the creature to the Creator.*

In the **Bible** the best relationship to God is that of reconciliation and peace with God.

The understanding of sin that is found in the **Koran** is such that sin is not against God but against the sinner himself. And since man is commanded to submit to God, God and man are never to be placed on the same rung. It follows that something such as reconciliation with God must not and cannot occur.

In the **Bible** God's reconciliation with man is of central importance. Mankind finds himself in an inimical relationship towards God (Romans 5:10; James 4:4). Still, in spite of the hostility, it is God's will to offer mankind reconciliation (Romans 3:20; 5:10; 2 Corinthians 5:15-21). The Old Testament points out how sin can be atoned for (Leviticus 4:5). In the center is the Day of Atonement which occurs once per year (Leviticus 16). The New Testament knows of only one atoning sacrifice, the sacrifice of Jesus Christ, who comprehensively atones for all guilt (Hebrews 9:12-28).

God is not the one who has to be reconciled. Rather, it is we who have to be reconciled. We have broken peace with God. It is not God who has broken peace with us. We have becomes God's enemies. It is not God who has become our enemy. The Scriptures refer to us when we read of those who were "enemies in your minds" (Colossians 1:21). For this reason Christ "put to death their hostility" (Ephesians 2:16). Mankind needs reconciliation, not God, and it is for this reason that Paul says: ". . . while we were God's enemies, we were reconciled to him" (Romans 5:10). At the same time, we do not reconcile ourselves to God. Rather, we are the recipients of God's reconciliation (Romans 5:11). "All this is from God, who reconciled us to himself through Christ and gave us the ministry of reconciliation: that God was reconciling the world to himself in Christ" (2 Corinthians 5: 18-19), and not the reverse. The central call of the gospel is therefore the summons: "Be reconciled to God" (2 Corinthians 5:20b). If this occurs, being a Christian means "peace with God" (Romans 5:1).

It is from the central relevance of reconciliation that the call to Christians to reconcile with other people draws its importance (1 Corinthians 7:11; Romans 12:18; 14:19; Ephesians 4:3; 1 Thessalonians 5:13; Hebrews 12:14; 1 Peter 3:11). Christian cultures are for that reason shaped by the concepts of reconciliation and forgiveness on all levels of society (between parents and children; nations toward each other), even if this is only done in a seemingly secular manner (e.g., between Germany and France after 1945).

III. Aids for Further Study

How can Christians Best Speak with Muslims?

The order of the day between Christians and Muslims is gentle, yet contentful and unambiguous discussions about belief in God – as was expressed well in the German Evangelical Church's title of its publication "Clarity and Being a Good Neighbor." Love and truth go hand in hand for Christians (2 John 1:3), because they want to "be truthful in love." This is also of great importance for the presentation of the Christian faith to those of opposing viewpoints, which has everything to do with a command in the New Testament and not a modern weakness.

From a Christian perspective there are always two sides of the coin to keep in mind that work together in a complementary manner:

A. Dialogue in the sense of a peaceful debate. Honest and patient listening and learning from others is a Christian virtue.

A dialogue between convinced Christians and followers of other religions is possible in the sense that Christians willingly speak with others about their faith ("... be prepared to give an answer to everyone ... But do this with gentleness and respect ....;" 1 Peter 3:15-16), listen willingly to others (James 1:19), learn about various aspects of life from the experiences of others (see the entire book of Proverbs), and are ready to repeatedly have themselves and their behavior challenged anew. Furthermore, the biblical command applies: "If it is possible, as far as it depends on you, live at peace with everyone" (Romans 12:18).

B. Dialogue in the sense of giving up Jesus' claim to truth or giving up the missionary witness is unthinkable without giving up Christianity itself.

If dialogue means to temporarily or principally suspend the innermost truth claims of Jesus Christ (John 14:6), of the gospel (Romans 1:16-17; 2:16), and of the salvific word of God (2 Timothy 3:16-17; Hebrews 4:12-13; John 17:17) in discussions with followers of other religions, or if it means to make such changes that leave the revelation of God in Christ and the revelation of the gospel in the Bible on the same rung as the revelations of other religions, then such a "dialogue" cannot be reconciled with the nature of Christianity and is not intellectually honest towards others.

Both principles belong together, because a critical position towards others and a gentle, respectful interaction with them are not mutually exclusive. When Paul defended himself in Athens in front of the philosophers of his time, it is written that "he was greatly distressed" to see the many idols in Athens (Acts 17:16). However, he still began his critical address with the words "Men of Athens! I see that in every way you are very religious" (Acts 17:22). How much more must that apply when Christians are in dialogue with followers of other monotheistic world religions!

The classical justification of any Christian "apologetic" (reasonable defense of the Christian faith) is found in 1 Peter 3:15b-16: "Always be prepared to give an answer to everyone who asks you to give the reason for the hope that you have. But do this with gentleness and respect, keeping a clear conscience, so that those who speak maliciously against your good behavior in Christ may be ashamed of their slander."

A complementarity can be clearly found here. On the one hand, there is the necessity of witness, if not of an apologetic (*apologia* means a defense plea before a court) and, on the other hand, there is "gentleness and respect," that is, true respect for the dignity of the other person. The dignity of people prevents Christians from concealing their hope. Rather, it leads to their articulating and explaining as well as defending. The same dignity prevents Christians from spurning the dignity of their partners in dialog, even when these questioners mean ill.

According to 1 Peter 3:15-16, people are not speaking directly with God when they speak with Christians. On the one hand Christians can definitely be ambassadors for God and bear witness to the hope that is in them. On the other hand, Christians are also only human beings, who are saved not by their own virtue but solely by the grace of God. Christians want to see people find peace with God, receive forgiveness, and trust God alone as the sole truth. But these people have not sinned against *us*, and they should not bow down before *us* and justify themselves. *We* are also not the ones who are the truth and who demonstrate the truth in *everything* that is said. Christians are not omniscient. They are normal people, who only possess special knowledge insofar as they testify to revealed truth in Jesus Christ and its history as recorded in the Bible.

Christians always view other people as images of God, even when they are of completely different points of view. In Christianity it is not from the fact that people are Christians that human rights are derived. Rather, it is due to the fact that they are men and women who are created by God and are all equal images of God. There are religions that only afford human rights to their own followers. Yet Christians also defend the human rights of their opponents – and then pray for them and love them.

In a time when extreme Islamists inflict violence on many Christians, it would be easy to simply point a finger at others and declare all Muslims virtually liable. Still, as we have seen, the Christian faith is very self-

III. Aids for Further Study

critical. We would like to speak in the manner of the Pharisee in Christ's parable: "God, I thank you that I am not like other men . . .," but according to Jesus' teaching we have to speak like the tax collector: "God, have mercy on me, a sinner" (Luke 18:11-13). As Christians our first question should not be: "What do other people do?" Rather, and even in the face of false accusations, we should ask ourselves: "Are we gentle and respectful to our fellow men?"

Gentleness is not only a mandatory consequence of the fact that we are proclaiming the God of love, and that we should, and desire to, love our neighbors. Rather, it is a consequence of the knowledge that we ourselves are pardoned sinners and not God. Our counterparts have to be reconciled with their Creator and not with us. For this reason we can always humbly step back and admit our own limitedness and inadequacies. This prevents us from treating someone as subhuman or as intellectually limited. Paul correctly admonishes: "Do not be proud ..." (Romans 12:16a). God's commandments and the commandments of men in a respective religious tradition and culture are kept strictly apart by Jesus (e.g., Mark 7:1-15). A Christian cannot come with the claim of knowing and representing the truth about *everything*. Rather, he is a fallible human being whose only pretense is that for which his counterpart is responsible before God, and this, only where God has himself commanded it.

Herein lies the danger for "Bible-believing" Christians, and that is that their "fundamentalism" (it does not matter if one likes the designation or not) is not confined to the contents of the message of Jesus Christ. It can become a loveless style that looks as if one knows it all. To be sure, Christians with a clear, dogmatic position have good opportunities in dialogs with Muslims, because a convinced Muslim would rather speak with a convinced Christian than with a rather "liberal" Christian, who does not know his own faith, or with an Atheist. For example, it is unfathomable for a convinced Muslim that a Christian theologian would deny the virgin birth of Jesus, even though this is taught in the New Testament (and in the Koran; Suras 3:19; 66:12). A dialog in the sense of a premature readiness to give up one's own doctrinal teachings and belief position, or a willingness to do the same out of niceness, is not at all called for by many Muslims. In any event such action is not at all respected.

The greatest opportunities that convinced Christians have in dialog with Muslims are destroyed when their style displays arrogance, pride, lovelessness, and a missing interest in their counterpart, or where they place politics or nationality over the personal encounter.

There is one more note to make regarding the commonalities between Christianity and Islam. When Muslims begin dialog with Christians, they often describe similarities. There is a problem with this, however: at that point they have said almost everything that is important to them. Christians, on the other hand, share such statements, but at that point have not said much about what is important to them. This is due to the fact that Christians do not simply believe in a Creator who desires that we do his will. Rather, Christians believe in a triune God, whose second person Jesus Christ achieved salvation for the world: He achieved salvation for the world because mankind is not able to free himself from the guilt of unrighteousness. It is precisely these things that are indispensable to Christians, and they do not appear in the list of similarities between Islam and Christianity.

Stated another way, if one lists the similarities, Muslims have said the majority of what is indispensable to them. Christians, on the other hand, have not mentioned what is most indispensable, since the similarity that we believe in a Creator completely ignores salvation in Jesus Christ.

Literature for Further Study

This book was originally published in German and is a result of discussions taking place within German and Turkish religious and academic groups. Therefore only part of the literature used and mentioned was in English.

The following list skips most of the German sources and adds some English sources. If you are interested in the original list of German literature, you can find it in Thomas Schirrmacher, *Koran und Bibel: Die größten Religionen im Vergleich*, Hänssler Verlag, 4th edition, 2012.

Non-Muslim Editions of the Koran and Non-Muslim Commentaries

http://quod.lib.umich.edu/k/koran/ (The University of Michigan Koran with good search options and modern language)

http://www.usc.edu/schools/college/crcc/engagement/resources/texts/muslim/quran/

quran.kiessecker.org (search functions in different translations of the Koran)

Muslim Editions of the Koran and Muslim Commentaries

http://www.islamicity.com/mosque/quran/ (with search functions)

www.quranexplorer.com/quran (text and sung/spoken Koran with many search options)

www.tafsir.com (Classic commentary with search options)

Further classical commentaries of the Koran can be find at the end of http://en.wikipedia.org/wiki/Tafsir

(Abdullah Yusuf Ali) The Holy Qur'an: English Translation of the Meanings and Commentary, Medina: King Fahd Holy Qur-an Printing, 1410 (= 1990)

Muslim Works on the Koran und Islam

www.unc.edu/~cernst/quranstudy.htm (Scientific sources in the web)

2nd chapter of Vol 1 of Sahih *al-Bukhari*, "The Book of Belief (Faith)", in: Sahih al-Bukhari Arabic-English, Vol. 1, ed. by Muhammad Muhsin

Khan, Kitab Bhavan, New Delhi, 1984, p.15-49 (also available in the internet, 2nd book of al-Bukhari, "Belief": http://www.usc.edu/dept/MSA/fundamentals/hadithsunnah/bukhari/

Bustami Mohamed *Khir*, "The Qur'an and Science: The Debate on the Validity of Scientific Interpretations," in: Colin *Turner*, Koran, pp. 297-312 [previously in *Journal of Qur'anic Studies* 2 (2000), pp. 19-35]

Geoffrey *Parrinder*, Jesus in the Qur'an, Oxford University Press: New York, 1977

Daud *Rahbar*, God of Justice, Leiden: Brill, 1960

Fazlur *Rahman*, Major Themes of the Qur'an, Minneapolis: Chicago, 1980

Abdullah *Saeed*, Interpreting the Qur'an, Routledge: London, 2005

Abdullah *Saeed*, Approaches to the Qur'an in Contemporary Indonesia, Oxford University Press: Oxford, 2006

Wazir Muhammad *Shaikh,* A Concise Dictionary of Islam: People and Places in the Holy Quran, Cosmo: New Delhi, 1998

Muhammad Zubayr *Siddiqi*, Hadith Literature: Its Origin, Development and Special Features, The Islamic Texts Society: Cambridge, 1993

Mokhtar *Stork*, A-Z Guide to the Qur'an, Singapore: Minaret Books/Time Books Int., 1999

W. Montgomery *Watt* (ed.), Islamic Creeds: A Selection, Edinburgh: Edinburgh University Press, 1994

Nonaligned and Academic Works Regarding the Koran and Islam

www.unc.edu/~cernst/quranstudy.htm (academic sources im web concerning Quran and Islam

de.wikipedia.org/wiki/Geschichte_des_Korantexts

The classic description of Muskim dogmatics (in German only) is: Hermann *Stieglecker*, Die Glaubenslehren des Islam, Paderborn: Schöningh, 1962-1, 1983-2

A. J. *Arberry*, Revelation and Reason in Islam, London: George Allen & Unwin Ltd, 1957

Dirk *Bakker*, Man in the Qur'an, Proefschrift Vrije Universiteit te Amsterdam: Amsterdam, 1965

Richard *Bell*, William M. *Watt*, Introduction to the Qur'ân, Edinburgh: University Press, 1970/1977

Josef *van Ess*, "Verbal Inspiration? Language and Revelation in Classical Islamic Theology", pp. 177-194 in: Stefan *Wild* (Hg.), The Qur'an as Text, Leiden: E. J. Brill, 1996

Harald *Motzki*, Introduction, in: Harald Motzki (ed.), Hadith. Origins and Developments, Ashgate Variorum: Aldershot 2004, pp. 13-63

F. E. *Peters*, Muhammad and the Origins of Islam, State University of New York Press: Albany, 1994

J. *Robson*, "Hadith" and "Hadith Qudsi", in: Encyclopaedia of Islam, Vol. III, E. J. Brill: Leiden, 1986, p. 23-29

Colin *Turner*, The Koran: Critical Concepts in Islamic Studies, London: RoutledgeCurzon, 2004

W. Montgomery *Watt* (ed.), Muhammad at Mecca, Oxford: Oxford University Press, 1953 (several reprints)

W. Montgomery *Watt* (ed.), Muhammad at Medina, Oxford: Oxford University Press, 1956 (several reprints)

A. T. *Welch*, J. D. *Pearson*, "al-Kur'an", in: Encyclopaedia of Islam, Vol. V, E. J. Brill: Leiden, 1986, pp. 400-432

Stefan *Wild* (Hg.), The Qur'an as Text, Leiden: E. J. Brill 1996

Dictionaries on Islam

Encyclopedia of Islam, 12 vol. Leiden: Brill 1960-2004 (also as CD-ROM and Internet version; the old German "Enzyklopädie des Islam" from 1926ff is out of date)

John L. *Esposito*, The Oxford Dictionary of Islam, Oxford University Press: Oxford, 2003

Hamilton Alexander Rosskeen *Gibb*, Johannes H. *Kramers*, Concise Encyclopedia of Islam, Boston: Brill, 2001

Richard C. *Martin*, Encyclopedia of Islam and the Muslim World, 2 vol., New York: Macmillan, 2004

Nonaligned and Academic Works Comparing the Bible and the Koran

Heribert *Busse*, Islam, Judaism and Christianity, Princeton (NJ): Markus Wiener Publ., 1998

Christine *Schirrmacher*, The Islamic View of Major Christian Teachings, Hamburg: RVB, 2001; 2009

Olaf *Schumann*, Jesus the Messiah in Muslim Thought, Delhi: ISPCK, 2002

Heinrich *Speyer*, Die biblischen Erzählungen im Qoran, Hildesheim: Georg Olms Verlag, 1988

Christian Works on the Koran and Islam and Comparisons of the Bible and the Koran

www.answering-islam.de

Brother *Mark*, A 'Perfect' Qur'an, n.p., 2000, see http://www.bible.ca/islam/library/perfect-koran/index.htm

William F. *Campbell*, The Quran and the Bible in the Light of History and Science, Upper Darby (PA): Middle East Resources, 1986

Mateen *Elsass*, Understanding the Koran, Grand Rapids (MI): Zondervan, 2004

Norman L. *Geisler*, Abdul *Saleeb*, Answering Islam, Baker: Grand Rapids (MI), 1994

Martin *Goldsmith*, Islam and Christian Witness, London: Hodder & Stoughton, 1982

Steven *Masood*, The Bible and the Quran: A Question of Integrity, Carlisle: OM, 2001

Chawkat *Moucarry*, Faith to Faith, Christianity and Islam in Dialogue, Intervarsity Press: Leicester, 2001

Christine *Schirrmacher*, "The Influence of Higher Bible Criticism on Muslim Apologetics in the Nineteenth Century," in: Jacques *Waardenburg,* Muslim Perceptions of Other Religions, Oxford University Press: New York/Oxford 1999, pp. 270-279)

Thomas *Schirrmacher*, "Bible and Koran as 'God's Word'", in: Islam und Christlicher Glaube/Islam and Christianity 6 (2005) 1: 11-15 (www.islaminstitut.de)

Thomas *Schirrmacher*, Feindbild Islam: Am Beispiel der Partei „Christliche Mitte", VTR: Nürnberg, 2003

Editions of the Bible

www.bibelserver.de / www.bibleserver.com

www.diebibel.de (twelve German translations as well as several other languages)

www.biblegateway.com (concordance to the Bible in 100 languages and other search tools)

http://bibletab.com/ (concordance to the Bible and other search tools)

The New Geneva Study Bible, Nashville (TN): Nelson, 1995; The Reformation Study Bible, 1998; The Reformation Study Bible (ESV), 2000

David H. *Stern*, Complete Jewish Bible, Jerusalem and Clarksville (MD): Jewish New Testament Publications, 1998

David H. *Stern*, Jewish New Testament Commentary, Jerusalem and Clarksville (MD): Jewish New Testament Publications, 1992

Muslim Works on the Bible and Christianity

Zakir *Naik*, The Qur'an and the Bible in the Light of Science: A Rejoinder to Dr. William Campbell's Comments, Faridabad: Baalaji Books, 2008

Introductions to the Bible and Christianity

Benedikt XVI – Joseph *Ratzinger*, Jesus of Nazareth, New York: Rizzoli, 2007

Craig L. *Blomberg*, Jesus and the Gospels, Nashville (TN): Broadman & Holman, 1997

Frank *Koppelin*, Thomas *Schirrmacher*, "The Gospels as Evidence of the Necessity for Cultural Adaptation in the Missionary Proclamation," MBS-Text 109 (2008), see also www.bucer.eu/86.html

Alister *McGrath*, Understanding the Trinity, Grand Rapids (MI): Zondervan, 1990

Alister *McGrath*, Christian Theology, Malden (MA): Blackwell, 2007

Jakob *van Bruggen*, The Future of the Bible, Nashville (TN): Thomas Nelson, 1978

On the Historical and Contemporary Relationship between Islam and Christianity

www.islaminstitut.de and its journal: *Islam und christlicher Glaube/Islam and Christianity*, since 1 (2001)

Habib *Badr*, Christianity: A History in the Middle East, Beirut: MECC, 2005

John L. *Esposito*, Democratization and Islam, Routledge: London, 2006

Jean-Marie *Gaudeul*, Called from Islam to Christ, Monarch: Crowborough, 1999

Jean-Marie *Gaudeul*, Encounters & Clashes : Islam and Christianity in History, 2 vol, Pontificio Istituto di Studi Arabi e Islamici: Rome, 1991

Hugh *Goddard*, A History of Christian-Muslim Relations, Edinburgh University Press: Edinburgh, 2000

Norman A. *Horner*, Rediscovering Christianity where it began, Beirut: Heidelberg Press, 1974

Bill *Musk*, The Unseen Face of Islam, Grand Rapisd (MI): Kregel, 2004

Christine *Schirrmacher,* Die Scharia, Holzgerlingen: Hänssler, 2007

Thomas *Schirrmacher*, Multikulturelle Gesellschaft, Holzgerlingen: Hänssler, 2006

Jacques *Waardenburg*, Islam: Historical, Social, and Political Perspectives, Berlin: de Gruyter, 2002

Bat *Ye'or*, The Decline of Eastern Christianity Under Islam From Jihad to Dhimmitude, Fairleigh Dickinson University Press: Madison (NJ), 1996

About the Author

Books by Thomas Schirrmacher in chronological order (With short commentaries)

For a full book list see www.thomasschirrmacher.net/eine-seite/books-published.

Selection from the author's books:

Theodor Christlieb und seine Missionstheologie. Verlag der Evangelischen Gesellschaft für Deutschland: Wuppertal, 1985. 308 pp.

[Theodor Christlieb and his theology of mission] *A study of the biography, theology and missiology of the leading German Pietist, professor of practical theology and international missions leader in the second half of the nineteenth century.*

Marxismus: Opium für das Volk? Schwengeler: Berneck (CH), 1990^1, 1997^2. 150 pp.

[Marxism: Opiate for the People?] *Marxism is proven to be a religion and an opiate for the masses. Empasizes the differences between Marxist and Biblical work ethics.*

Paul in Conflict with the Veil!? VTR: Nürnberg, 2002^1; 2007^2. 130 pp.

Exegetical examination of 1. Corinthians 11,2-16, following an alternative view of John Lightfoot, member of the Westminster assembly in the 16th century.

Ethik. Neuhausen: Hänssler, 1994^1. 2 vol. 883 & 889 pp.; Hamburg: RVB & Nürnberg: VTR, 2001^2. 3 vol. 2150 pp.; 2002^3, 2009^4; 2011^5. 8 volumes. 2850 pp.

[Ethics] Major Evangelical ethics in German covering all aspects of general, special, persocial and public ethics.

Legends About the Galilei-Affair. RVB International: Hamburg, 2001^1; 2008.^{2}. 120 pp.

Law or Spirit? An Alternative View of Galatians. RVB International: Hamburg, 2001^1; 2008.^{2}. 160 pp.

This commentary emphasising the ethical aspects of Galatians wants to prove that Galatians is not only fighting legalists but also a second party of Paul's opponents, who were totally opposed to the Old Testament and the Law.

God Wants You to Learn, Labour and Love. Reformation Books: Hamburg, 1999. 120 pp.

Four essays for Third World Christian Leaders on Learning with Jesus, Work Ethic, Love and Law and Social Involvement.

World Mission – Heart of Christianity. RVB International: Hamburg, 1999^1; 2008.^{2}. 120 pp.

Articles on the Biblical and systematic fundament of World Mission, especially on mission as rooted in God's being, on 'Mission in the OT', and 'Romans as a Charter for World Mission'.

Human Rights Threatened in Europe: Euthanasia – Abortion – Bioethicconvention. RVB International: Hamburg, 2001^1; 2008.^{2}. 100 pp.

Updated Lectures on euthanasia and biomedicine at the 1st European Right to Life Forum Berlin, 1998, and articles on abortion.

Be Keen to Get Going: William Careys Theology. RVB: Hamburg, 2001[1]; 2008[2]. 64 pp.

First discussion of Carey's theology in length, explaining his Calvinistic and Postmillenial backround.

Love is the Fulfillment of Love – Essays in Ethics. RVB: Hamburg, 2001[1]; 2008[2]. 140 pp.

Essays on ethical topics, including role of the Law, work ethics, and European Union.

Mission und der Kampf um die Menschenrechte. RVB: Hamburg, 2001. 108 S.

[Mission and the Battle for Human Rights] *The relationship of world missions and the fight for human rights is discussed on an ethical level (theology of human rights) as well as on a practical level.*

The Persecution of Christians Concerns Us All: Towards a Theology of Martyrdom. At the same time Idea-Dokumentation 15/99 E. VKW: Bonn, 2001. 156 pp.

70 thesis on persecution and martyrdom, written for the International Day of Prayer for the Persecuted Church on behalf of the German and European Evangelical Alliance

Hope for Europe: 66 Theses. VTR: Nürnberg, 2002

Official thesis and study of hope in the Old and New Testament for Hope for Europe of the European Ev. Alliance and Lausanne Europe. Also available in German, Czech, Dutch, Spanish, Romanian, Portuguese, French, Russian, Italian, Hungarian, Latvian.

Thomas Schirrmacher, Christine Schirrmacher u. a. Harenberg Lexikon der Religionen. Harenberg Verlag: Düsseldorf, 2002. 1020 pp.

[Harenberg Dictionary of World Religions] In a major secular dictionary on world religions, Thomas Schirrmacher wrote the section on Christianity ('Lexicon of Christianity', pp. 8-267) and Christine Schirrmacher the section on Islam ('Lexicon of Islam', 'pp. 428-549).

Studies in Church Leadership: New Testament Church Structure – Paul and His Coworkers – An Alternative Theological Education – A Critique of Catholic Canon Law. VKW: Bonn, 2003[1]; RVB: Hamburg, 2008.[2]. 112 pp.

Hitlers Kriegsreligion: Die Verankerung der Weltanschauung Hitlers in seiner religiösen Begrifflichkeit und seinem Gottesbild. 2 vol. VKW: Bonn, 2007. 1220 pp.

[Hitlers Religion of War] *A research about the religious terms and thoughts in all texts and speeches of Hitler of Hitler, pleading for a new way of explaining Hitler's worldview, rise and breakdown.*

Moderne Väter: Weder Waschlappen, noch Despot. Hänssler: Holzgerlingen, 2007. 96 pp.

[Modern Fathers] Presents the result of international father research, explains the necessity of the father's involvement for his children and gives practical guidelines.

Internetpornografie. Hänssler: Holzgerlingen, 2008. 156 pp.

[Internet pornography] *Intense study of spread of pornography, its use amongst children and young people,* its *psychological results and dangers, including steps how to escape sex and pornography addiction.*

May a Christian Go to Court and other Essays on Persecution vs. Religious Freedom. WEA Global Issues Series. VKW: Bonn, 2008. 120 pp.

Essays: "Is Involvement in the Fight Against the Persecution of Christians Solely for the Benefit of Christians?", "But with gentleness and respect: Why missions should be ruled by ethics". "May a Christian Go to Court?", "Putting Rumors to Rest", "Human Rights and Christian Faith", "There Has to Be a Social Ethic".

Indulgences: A History of Theology and Reality of Indulgences and Purgatory. VKW: Bonn, 2011. 164 pp.

History and theology of the Catholic view on indulgences.

Thomas Schirrmacher, Richard Howell. Racism. With an essay on Caste in India. VKW: Bonn, 2011. 100 pp.

History and scientific errors of racism

Menschenrechte: Anspruch und Wirklichkeit. Holzgerlingen: SCM Hänssler, 2012. 120 pp.

[Human Rights]: *Ethical arguments for human rights versus the present stage of the violation of human rights worldwide.*

Christ and the Trinity in the Old Testament. Edited by James E. Anderson. RVB: Hamburg, 2013. 82 pp.

On Christ and the Trinity in the Old Testament and on 'the Angel of the Lord'. Taken from 'Ethik'.

Selection from the books edited by the author:

Scham- und Schuldorientierung in der Diskussion: Kulturanthropologische, missiologische und theologische Einsichten (mit Klaus W. Müller). VTR: Nürnberg & VKW: Bonn, 2006

[Shame- and Guiltorientation] *A selection of experts from all continents on the difference between shame- and guiltoriented cultures and its implications for world missions.*

HIV und AIDS als christliche Herausforderung (mit Kurt Bangert). Verlag für Kultur und Wissenschaft: Bonn, 2008. 211 pp.

[HIV and AIDS as Christian Challenge] *Essay on how the Christian church should react to HIV and AIDS and how it does react. Published together with World Vision Germany.*

Der Kampf gegen die weltweite Armut – Aufgabe der Evangelischen Allianz? Zur biblisch-theologischen Begründung der Micha-Initiative. (with Andreas Kusch). VKW/Idea: Bonn, 2009. 230 pp.

[The fight against poverty – task of the Evangelical Alliance?] *Essays by theologians, missiologists, activists etc. in favour of the MICAH initiative of the World Evangelical Alliance.*

Tough-Minded Christianity: Honoring the Legacy of John Warwick Montgomery. (with William Dembski). (2009) B&H Academic Publ.: Nashville (TN). 830 pp.

Large Festschrift with essays by many major Evangelical theologians and lawyers.

Calvin and World Mission: Essays- VKW: Bonn, VTR: Nürnberg, 2009. 204 pp.

Collection of essays from 1882 to 2002.

Biography

Prof. Dr. theol. Dr. phil. Thomas Schirrmacher, PhD, ThD, DD (born 1960), serves the World Evangelical Alliance [networking 600 million Protestants] as Associate Secretary General for Theological Concerns (responsible for Theology, Intrafaith and Interfaith Relations, Religious Freedom and Persecution) and as Chair of its Theological Commission.

As President of the International Council of the International Society for Human Rights (with sections in 55 countries), and as Director of the International Institute for Religious Freedom (Bonn, Cape Town, Colombo, São Paulo), Schirrmacher is one of the leading experts on human rights worldwide and regularly testifies in parliaments and courts worldwide, the OSCE and the UN in Geneva and New York.

Schirrmacher is visiting professor of the sociology of religion at the state University of the West in Timisoara (Romania) and Distinguished Professor of Global Ethics and International Development at William Carey University in Shillong (Meghalaya, India). He is president of 'Martin Bucer European Theological Seminary' (Bonn, Berlin, Prague, Istanbul, São Paulo), where he teaches ethics and comparative religions.

He studied theology from 1978 to 1982 at STH Basel (Switzerland) and since 1983 Cultural Anthropology and Comparative Religions at Bonn State University. He earned a Drs. theol. in Missiology and Ecumenics at Theological University (Kampen/Netherlands) in 1984, and a Dr. theol. in Missiology and Ecumenics at Johannes Calvin Foundation (Kampen/Netherlands) in 1985, a Ph.D. in Cultural Anthropology at Pacific Western University in Los Angeles (CA) in 1989, a Th.D. in Ethics at Whitefield Theological Seminary in Lakeland (FL) in 1996, and a Dr. phil. in Sociology of Religion at State University of Bonn in 2007. In 1997 he received an honorary doctorate (D.D.) from Cranmer Theological House, in 2006 one from Acts University in Bangalore.

His has authored and edited 102 books, which were translated into 17 languages, his newest dealing with 'Suppressed Women' (2015), 'Corruption' (2014), 'Human Rights' (2012), 'Human trafficking' (2011), 'Fundamentalism' (2010) and 'Racism' (2009).

He is listed in Marquis' Who's Who in the World, Dictionary of International Biography, International Who is Who of Professionals, 2000 Outstanding Intellectuals of the 21st Century, Kürschners Gelehrten-Kalender and other biographical year-books.

World Evangelical Alliance

World Evangelical Alliance is a global ministry working with local churches around the world to join in common concern to live and proclaim the Good News of Jesus in their communities. WEA is a network of churches in 129 nations that have each formed an evangelical alliance and over 100 international organizations joining together to give a worldwide identity, voice and platform to more than 600 million evangelical Christians. Seeking holiness, justice and renewal at every level of society – individual, family, community and culture, God is glorified and the nations of the earth are forever transformed.

Christians from ten countries met in London in 1846 for the purpose of launching, in their own words, "a new thing in church history, a definite organization for the expression of unity amongst Christian individuals belonging to different churches." This was the beginning of a vision that was fulfilled in 1951 when believers from 21 countries officially formed the World Evangelical Fellowship. Today, 150 years after the London gathering, WEA is a dynamic global structure for unity and action that embraces 600 million evangelicals in 129 countries. It is a unity based on the historic Christian faith expressed in the evangelical tradition. And it looks to the future with vision to accomplish God's purposes in discipling the nations for Jesus Christ.

Commissions:

- Theology
- Missions
- Religious Liberty
- Women's Concerns
- Youth
- Information Technology

Initiatives and Activities

- Ambassador for Human Rights
- Ambassador for Refugees
- Creation Care Task Force
- Global Generosity Network
- International Institute for Religious Freedom
- International Institute for Islamic Studies
- Leadership Institute
- Micah Challenge
- Global Human Trafficking Task Force
- Peace and Reconciliation Initiative
- UN-Team

Church Street Station
P.O. Box 3402
New York, NY 10008-3402
Phone +[1] 212 233 3046
Fax +[1] 646-957-9218
www.worldea.org

Giving Hands

GIVING HANDS GERMANY (GH) was established in 1995 and is officially recognized as a nonprofit foreign aid organization. It is an international operating charity that – up to now – has been supporting projects in about 40 countries on four continents. In particular we care for orphans and street children. Our major focus is on Africa and Central America. GIVING HANDS always mainly provides assistance for self-help and furthers human rights thinking.

The charity itself is not bound to any church, but on the spot we are co-operating with churches of all denominations. Naturally we also cooperate with other charities as well as governmental organizations to provide assistance as effective as possible under the given circumstances.

The work of GIVING HANDS GERMANY is controlled by a supervisory board. Members of this board are Manfred Feldmann, Colonel V. Doner and Kathleen McCall. Dr. Christine Schirrmacher is registered as legal manager of GIVING HANDS at the local district court. The local office and work of the charity are coordinated by Rev. Horst J. Kreie as executive manager. Dr. theol. Thomas Schirrmacher serves as a special consultant for all projects.

Thanks to our international contacts companies and organizations from many countries time and again provide containers with gifts in kind which we send to the different destinations where these goods help to satisfy elementary needs. This statutory purpose is put into practice by granting nutrition, clothing, education, construction and maintenance of training centers at home and abroad, construction of wells and operation of water treatment systems, guidance for self-help and transportation of goods and gifts to areas and countries where needy people live.

GIVING HANDS has a publishing arm under the leadership of Titus Vogt, that publishes human rights and other books in English, Spanish, Swahili and other languages.

These aims are aspired to the glory of the Lord according to the basic Christian principles put down in the Holy Bible.

Baumschulallee 3a • D-53115 Bonn • Germany
Phone: +49 / 228 / 695531 • Fax +49 / 228 / 695532
www.gebende-haende.de • info@gebende-haende.de

Martin Bucer Seminary

**Faithful to biblical truth
Cooperating with the Evangelical Alliance
Reformed**

Solid training for the Kingdom of God
- Alternative theological education
- Study while serving a church or working another job
- Enables students to remain in their own churches
- Encourages independent thinking
- Learning from the growth of the universal church.

Academic
- For the Bachelor's degree: 180 Bologna-Credits
- For the Master's degree: 120 additional Credits
- Both old and new teaching methods: All day seminars, independent study, term papers, etc.

Our Orientation:
- Complete trust in the reliability of the Bible
- Building on reformation theology
- Based on the confession of the German Evangelical Alliance
- Open for innovations in the Kingdom of God

Our Emphasis:
- The Bible
- Ethics and Basic Theology
- Missions
- The Church

Our Style:
- Innovative
- Relevant to society
- International
- Research oriented
- Interdisciplinary

Structure
- 15 study centers in 7 countries with local partners
- 5 research institutes
- President: Prof. Dr. Thomas Schirrmacher
  Vice President: Prof. Dr. Thomas K. Johnson
- Deans: Thomas Kinker, Th.D.;
  Titus Vogt, lic. theol., Carsten Friedrich, M.Th.

Missions through research
- Institute for Religious Freedom
- Institute for Islamic Studies
- Institute for Life and Family Studies
- Institute for Crisis, Dying, and Grief Counseling
- Institute for Pastoral Care

www.bucer.eu • info@bucer.eu
**Berlin I Bielefeld I Bonn I Chemnitz I Hamburg I Munich I Pforzheim
Innsbruck I Istanbul I Izmir I Linz I Prague I São Paulo I Tirana I Zurich**

www.ingramcontent.com/pod-product-compliance
Lightning Source LLC
Chambersburg PA
CBHW070325100426
42743CB00011B/2569